THINK GOOD THOUGHTS

J.P. (PAT) LYNCH

iUniverse, Inc.
Bloomington

Think Good Thoughts

iUniverse books may be ordered through booksellers or by contacting:

iUniverse
1663 Liberty Drive
Bloomington, IN 47403
www.iuniverse.com
1-800-Authors (1-800-288-4677)

ISBN: 978-1-4502-6806-6 (pbk)
ISBN: 978-1-4502-7056-4 (ebk)

Printed in the United States of America

iUniverse rev. date: 12/18/10

To Wanda and the other warriors on all sides of the fight against a scary enemy, including those who can only stand on the sidelines and hope to be able to help.

My special thanks to Cathy for her assistance with this endeavour.

These thoughts and words were put together when the emotions were very raw. I hope, however, that you enjoy some of the stories.

PREFACE

It will become evident very quickly to anyone reading these stories, memories and comments that I am not a professional writer. I may be a better than average observer. I believe I can tell stories reasonably well.

I've tried to take this tale or short history through to a reader as I saw it and as it was dealt with by me. It is not an instruction booklet nor is it intended to be "preachy".

We were told that Wanda has cancer. It's a terrifying word and it came as a shock to two people who have lived a fortunate life and who believed that today's seventy is yesterday's fifty.

I just tried to convey how things hit me and how I tried to either face them or, in one way or another, drive them away.

I also wanted to tell of the wonderful people that we have encountered on this journey. I tried to do this, in part, by recalling the great memories and fun times that we shared with our friends and with each other.

How another person handles this type of situation will probably be totally different than what I was able to. Wanda and I talk a lot. I told her, immediately after we learned there was a problem, that I will probably do and say a lot of things and I won't always get them right. Sometimes I will get them totally wrong.

I would like to hope that if anything comes from this collection of stories, observations and memories that it will help someone somewhere get it more right than I was able to do. If you are on such a journey we wish you well. If it helps you understand that your feelings are similar to those of someone else in the same situation, then perhaps I have done the right thing in putting my thoughts on paper.

My choice of the title "Think Good Thoughts" is the closest I will come to giving advice.

What a Way to Meet

When I was seventeen years old I had pretty much given up on girls and they had pretty much given up on me.

I found they were expensive and my fourteen dollars a week in spending money didn't go nearly far enough and as a seventeen year old healthy male with raging hormones I didn't get to go nearly far enough either.

I needed something in my life that had some real meaning. Something that made real sense. Something reliable.

Baseball. That was it. Baseball.

It had been around for over a hundred years. The bases were still the same distances apart. The pitchers mound was the same distance as it ever was from the plate. There were still four balls and three strikes. You still needed to get three outs in an inning. When you hit the ball you still ran in the same direction and then continued from base to base just like it had always been done. There was no time limit. You always had a chance to win until the last man was out. You ran. You jumped. You caught. You slid. You did all those things without wondering what you're supposed to do next. That sure made it different from that girl thing that usually left you totally confused and close to broke after most encounters. Baseball was reliable.

So, I decided to give up on the girls and concentrate on baseball. You never know. I was fast. I had good hands. I had good baseball sense and played a pretty mean shortstop. Maybe I could even make it as a professional baseball player. Mind you, this is the same guy who once in his life shot an eighty-one playing a mini golf course and came home and announced that I was certain that with a little more practice I could become a professional golfer. For the record, anyone who ever watched me swing a golf club knows what a laugher of an idea that had been.

But girls were off the agenda and baseball was on.

I wound up playing for a team in the Catholic Youth Organization that played in a schoolyard and the game was then followed up with a CYO dance in the nearby Church Hall. When the game was over I just packed up my stuff and went home. As I had given up on girls the dance was of no interest to me so I went home and watched our black and white TV and checked all four available channels to see if there was a baseball game being televised. It was a life that made good sense to me and I was also able to contribute a few extra bucks to the family pot because I hadn't spent all my pay on those girls that I mentioned earlier.

The plan was holding together beautifully for about a month. I still couldn't hit but I was playing a better game, at shortstop, than ever before. Then things came apart.

My good friend Ted, who was on the same team as me, told me he had met a girl at the CYO dance a couple of weeks before and insisted that I should meet her as she was the type of girl I would really like. I thanked him for his concern over my social life but declined the honour. The following week he again insisted that I should meet this person. Again, I declined with thanks. The following week he again insisted that I should meet the mystery girl. As I knew there was nothing good on TV that night I gave it up, went to the dance and was introduced to Wanda.

Wow.

I had left school the previous year. I had a job and I had a car. I figured that with a job and a car I had a chance of making some kind of favourable impression on this person I had just met and being brave of heart I asked her if I could drive her home and perhaps stop for a coffee. She thought that might be a nice idea provided that I also drove her brother home with us as he was also at the dance. I also learned that night that neither one of them knew the first thing about baseball and could care less. Here I was meeting a major part of the family, seeing the brother as a chaperone and discovering that they don't know a thing about baseball and thinking, " That's okay. I can deal with this."

It took me three weeks before I told her we should plan on getting married. It took me three years to close the deal and to get our "I do" responses said in front of an old priest at St. Lawrence's Church in the north end of Hamilton.

At this writing we are coming up on our fifty-third wedding anniversary this summer. Three children, two grandchildren, four houses, a bankruptcy, some great traveling, golf at one of the best courses in the country, ups, downs, hurts and joys but what a great decision I made when I went to a CYO dance instead of going home and watching TV. By the way, Ted and his wife Marianne stood up for us at our wedding and we stood up for them at theirs.

Now, I probably came as close to messing this thing up as I ever did when I sneaked out of our wedding reception and went to the hotel next door to watch a ball game that was on TV. It was a small reception so it wasn't long before I was missed by the new bride. Someone ratted me out. I think it was Ted.

When I explained to Wanda that the Boston Red Sox were playing and that Ted Williams was in the line-up, she saw the importance of my decision. Marriage can be a test.

An Envelope on the Table

Wanda and I have been married for fifty-three years at this writing.

Most of that time we made every effort to eat breakfast and dinner together. We did that before we had kids and continued the practice when we had the three little darlings. Big Macs and five different menus or five different mealtimes were never our style. We sat the kids down and actually made every effort to exchange information about the day to come or about the day just past. Breakfast was in the kitchen and dinner was in the dining room, when we had a dining room.

When we bought our first house we had three mortgages and I had one job for each mortgage. The only way we could qualify for the major mortgage was to build a four bedroom house. The only way we could build a four bedroom house was to drywall over the doorway that led from the kitchen to the dining room until the mortgage inspection was done and the dining room was counted as a bedroom. We had framed the doorway between the two rooms before it was dry walled so that we could cut through the drywall and open up the door space after the inspections were finished.

Our contractor told us he would cut the opening for us for only thirty dollars. We told him to come back in three months as it would take us that long to save up all that money. For three months we walked out of the kitchen through the living room and then into our fourth bedroom/dining room. It made good sense at the time and, by God, we were eating in our dining room.

The kitchen table always seemed to be covered with stuff. We always had a small wicker basket on the table and tossed in bills to be paid, notices, statements, brochures that we would never look at again and unopened envelopes among other bits and pieces. From time to time we cleared out the basket.

During one such clear-out I noticed an unopened envelope and asked Wanda about it.

"It's just a reminder that I'm due for a breast screening and I haven't arranged it yet but I will."

We always ate dinner in the dining room. When we lived on a farm and had a couple of old horses for the kids, Wanda and I would sit at the table and yak to each other after dinner about the day or whatever. Wanda's chair faced the patio doors and she could see what was happening on the farm. Our eldest daughter would go out to the barn and saddle a great little appaloosa named Joel and take him for a ride. The two of them would gallop up the rather steep hills until Tammara started to slip. The horse, being endowed with more horse-sense than the rider, would immediately slow until Tammara regained her balance and continued the ride.

Wanda would watch this scene taking place over my shoulder and would wince or mouth, "look outs" and "be carefuls" as the game played out. I finally told her that she either needs to control her panics caused by the daughter and the horse or we need to switch chairs.

We always ate dinner in the dining room and we still do. The horse never stumbled and Tammara never fell off. At least not when Wanda was looking.

Who Am I?

When we first moved into Ancaster we were part of that great migration that headed into the suburbs. We had the common interests of mortgages, children of the same age, new or changing careers and no money. The term "disposable income" was not yet invented or, if it had been, it had little or no meaning to us or to our neighbours.

A two car family was considered to either be very rich or clearly living beyond their means. Entertainment came from the Bring Your Own Bottle Saturday night barbeque with the neighbours, from the Church Bowling League, from the neighbourhood basement Ping Pong league or from one of the local Service Clubs.

I tried them all and failed miserably. I was even asked to resign from a local Service Club because I laughed too hard and too long the night they were scheduled to reward someone with a twenty-five year perfect attendance button and the recipient wasn't there. As I was being ushered out of the meeting hall I took the position once taken by Groucho Marx when he announced that he wanted nothing to do with any club that would have him as a member.

I decided to stay away from clubs for a while. Fifty years later I was persuaded by some of my friends to join a club that was really a meeting place for retired or semi-retired men to meet and hear about what is taking place in the community. It was a pleasant get together most of the time and even though I was seventy-three at the time, I enjoyed hearing people call me "son".

One of the requirements that go with the membership is the ritual of standing up before the club membership and giving them a run down of your life and of your achievements. I've looked upon this task with the same good feelings that I've had about serving on jury duty. As a matter of fact, President Obama and myself share one thing in common; we've both been excused from jury duty because of other more pressing commitments. In his case he had to run a country. In my case we had a health situation that needed to be attended to.

However, in anticipation of a time to come when I will need to tell my life's story I thought I should jot down a little about myself and present it in much the same way as I would present my tale of life to my fellow club members.

I would need to tell them that after hearing other members tell their stories and learning about their lives as lawyers, judges, business tycoons, Hall of Fame athletes, inventors and so forth, I came to the realization that I really had done nothing of any importance so I really had nothing to report.

Sure, I could tell them that I was born in the hard rock gold mining town of Timmins, Ontario and came to Hamilton as a young man. Actually, I made that decision when I was five years old and my father said to me, "Get in the car kid. We're moving to Hamilton."

I could tell them I was married to Wanda in 1957 and we had three children all of whom, at this writing, have stayed out of jail. I worked in the hotel business where I met a contractor from the U.S. who was opening a branch of their business in Canada. He hired me to run his office and eventually we bought the Canadian arm of the company and ran it for over twenty-five years.

I could tell them that I was the campaign manager for several federal politicians who went to Ottawa, for good or for bad. I could tell them I spent two years on a school board, bought a farm and raised beef cattle and horses.

I could tell them I went broke during a recession and came back from that to build a solid financial planning business with my son Dan.

None of this can stack up against the accomplishments of my fellow club members so I've been at a loss for speech materials and I've avoided the challenge to date as I really felt I had done nothing of much importance in comparison to those who have already spoken.

Then I thought, "Wait a minute. I wrote my stories down for my children and grandchildren to read and, perhaps, to wonder about." I put them together in a book and passed the stories along. That is very important.

Everyone has these stories to tell. Sometimes we pass them along but all too often we do not. Anyone can write them down so that some person on another day can feel somewhat like you felt when you made yourself, or someone else, laugh, cry or change just a little bit. That, I believe, is quite an accomplishment and it just may stand up with bigger and better things done by so many others.

I would then read them the story of how I handled a situation with a stray beagle hound and made a complete fool of myself. That's for another time.

Hang on to Your Fork

When the kids were quite small we decided to take a driving trip to the Maritimes and to spend some time on Prince Edward Island.

Wanda is from New Brunswick and came down to Hamilton as a young girl following the urging of her older brother Jim. Jim had left New Brunswick and came to Hamilton at the age of seventeen to find work and to help support his mother and three younger sisters. His father had drifted off somewhere and it fell on him to support the family. As Wanda reached the age where she could legally leave school, she too took up part of the weight that comes from raising a family. There was little work in New Brunswick at the time so Jim got a job at the Fuller Brush Company and moved the family to Ontario.

Wanda very reluctantly left school and picked up her part of the load working at a local bank. Most of the money she earned went into the family coffers and they made due.

Our trip to the Maritimes was primarily one of curiosity on my part and one of re-visiting on the part of Wanda. As far as the kids were concerned, they just got into the car and went where we went.

The night before we left on our trip, Dan complained about an insect bite on his knee. It was slightly swollen and we gave him the advice of "Don't scratch it. You'll be fine." By the time we got to Quebec City it was badly swollen and we dealt with that information by making the observation, "You must be scratching it. Leave it alone and you'll be fine." Dan was always a tough little guy and we didn't hear much from him about the problem but he was limping along when we walked anyplace.

When we got to Wanda's old home town of Campbellton, New Brunswick, she was amazed at how much it had shrunk since she was there as a kid. Thomas Wolfe once said, "You can't go home again". When you visit a town or a school that you have not seen since childhood it's clear, in part, what Thomas Wolfe met. The hills you coasted down as a terror filled child are now half the height. The streets are shorter between your house and your school. The house you lived in is much smaller. The Town Hall and the Police Station are both much less imposing.

I was more interested in seeing the Restigouche River that ran through the area. The Restigouche was always famous for the salmon fish it produced. It became so famous, in fact, that the entire riverfront had been purchased over the years by the rich and the famous so that they could have exclusive use of the Restigouche and have exclusive rights to fish the river. That situation exists to this day.

I suppose that the New Brunswickers that cannot get a job working in one of the fishing "camps" owned by the R&F could always move to Hamilton and get jobs working for the Fuller Brush Company or a bank. Just don't get caught fishing in the river that runs past your town.

An ex-New Brunswicker friend of mine told me the story of a guide that had a party of R&F guests out on the river fishing when he spotted an elderly man sneaking along the banks of the Restigouche with a fishing rod in his hand.

The guide, knowing he had the fully protected rights to use the Restigouche, started yelling at the man to get away from the river and let him know in no uncertain terms that he had no right to be on the property reserved for the excusive use of the R&F. He punctuated his comments by throwing a few well aimed rocks at the elderly fisherman.

One of the guest fishermen remarked that the guide was particularly aggressive about chasing the man away.

"He knows better than to be there," said the guide.

"How do you know that he was even aware of the rules?" asked the fisherman.

"Because, he's my father," answered the guide. "He should know better than to try to get away with that kind of sneakiness."

So much for our visit to Campbellton. We moved on to Prince Edward Island. P.E.I. is beautiful. Every hilltop presents another calendar view. At the time we visited "the Island" there was no Causeway to carry traffic. There was an excellent Ferry Boat service that added a sailing adventure to the trip for the kids and that left one with the feeling that you were really in a different place once you landed on P.E.I.

We didn't golf at that time so we just enjoyed the people, the scenery, the beaches and the food. We also kept telling Dan to stop scratching his knee and to limp faster so that he could keep up.

One of the main features of P.E.I. at that time, and apparently, still is, is the Church Lobster Suppers. Most Churches on the island offered a great Lobster Dinner complete with home cooked potatoes, salads and other veggies and your choice of home baked pie. The cooking was all done by the Church ladies and the food was served by high school age girls. It brought in a few dollars for the community and it provided a good summer job for some of the young locals. It was great food. It was served very plainly on long tables with paper plates and there wasn't much left at the end of the meal.

The young waitresses looked after their visitors as best they could. Most were working at their very first job but they made a great effort to be as friendly and helpful as possible.

As we enjoyed the meal, the people and the atmosphere it reminded me of a story that made the rounds following a visit that Prince Phillip had made to Western Canada. He was treated to a similar style meal in a Church basement in a small town somewhere out west. After the main course had been served and the young waitresses were clearing the tables, one of them was reputed to have said to Prince Phillip,

"You better hang onto your fork Your Princeship. We're having pie for dessert."

I hope it's a true story. I like to tell it at dinners where there are numerous knives and forks laid out and I'm always surprised at how many people let the wait staff take them all away and then need to ask for another fork for their pie.

We did our trip of P.E.I. We intend to go back next year and bring the golf clubs.

We made an unscheduled stop in Campbellton on our way back so that we could take Dan into the local hospital to have his knee lanced open to drain what had become a serious infection from a spider bite. He obviously had a right to limp.

He now has no trouble killing spiders even if it might make it rain.

Just Lunch

Someone once told me that if you have staff working for you, it's very important that you look after them in the way that usually works best.

Feed them.

We have great people working for us and we have very little turn-over of staff. We like to believe that our success with staff comes from the fact that we feed them.

Wanda is often included in these little get-togethers as she has always played a part in our business successes and is a good person to have around at a lunch or dinner. Wanda has always worked on the theory that nature abhors a vacuum and considers silence around a luncheon table to be a vacuum. Naturally, such a vacuum needs to be immediately filled with good chat.

It was a nice, warm August day, one of the few delightful weather days we had that summer. We had invented some excuse to have an office lunch on a nearby patio. Wanda joined us.

She seemed somewhat pre-occupied.

"What's bothering you," I asked.

"The clinic called this morning and they want me to go back and have something re-checked."

"What's going on?"

"They said something showed up on that screening I had done and they want to re-take the pictures and maybe do a biopsy. I have an appointment at two today."

"I'll go with you", I said.

I'm On the Radio

Stuart McLean does an excellent weekly radio show on the Canadian Broadcasting Corporation called the Vinyl Café. It's a show of little stories about fictional characters invented by Stuart McLean and it goes coast to coast across Canada.

One of the features of the show comes through his reading stories that have been submitted by the listening public. As I had written a number of my stories and formed them into a book, I thought I would submit the book to Stuart and let him judge whether or not any of my tales were worth using.

A short time after I had submitted the book I received a call from one of his assistants. She informed me that Stuart had really enjoyed my story about a stray beagle hound and wanted to know if I would give him permission to use the story on his show.

I was flattered and thrilled and, of course, agreed to sign the release that would allow him to use the story. I was told he would use the story at one of his live shows to be taped for radio use and it would play in three weeks on his show.

To bring you up to speed, the story was about the day Wanda and I moved into our new home in Ancaster. That was the house with three mortgages that I was paying for by holding three jobs.

We were unpacking with the front door wide open and a little beagle hound, tail wagging, walked right in. I knew our new neighbours across the street owned a beagle hound that they kept in their basement when they were out. As I knew they were out for the evening, I assumed the dog somehow had escaped and wandered into our place.

Wanting to be a good neighbour and wanting to make a good first impression I thought the best thing to do would be to take the dog across the street and, if the basement door was unlocked, return him to his rightful owners in his rightful home.

I picked up the dog, crossed the street, found the basement door unlocked and deposited the beagle in the basement.

Much to my shock, the darndest dog fight broke out that I had ever heard as their dog was already in the basement and I had just deposited a second dog into the mix. As, obviously, I had no idea how to tell one of them from the other I just made a break for home and told Wanda to turn out the lights and lock the door. So much for my start as a good neighbour.

Apparently the story just broke up Stuart McLean and he was to use it on his show from somewhere in Saskatchewan.

Well, I was pretty excited and pumped up about some of my material being used on a nationally broadcast show. I told all my friends. I told my relatives. I told my clients. "Saturday at 10:30, listen to Stuart McLean."

I had a tape machine hooked up and ready to go. I had Wanda sitting in the living room giving this her undivided and rapt attention. I was about to be a somebody.

On came the Vinyl Café. On came Stuart McLean. On came my story.

The good people in the live audience in Saskatchewan seemed to very much enjoy the story and the reading of it. They laughed at all the right places and I just sat and became more and more full of myself as the show went on.

When the segment was finished I said to Wanda, "What do you think about that? Does that make me a somebody, or what"?

"I'll tell you what I think about that", she said in her quiet way.

"Up until now, only your family and a few of your close friends knew that you were a balloon head. Now, with this going coast to coast, everyone in the country knows."

Isn't it nice to get solid support from home?

Marigolds Are Nice

When we are young we often do really stupid things. When we are old we often do stupid things but not quite as many.

Catholics believe that it's necessary to confess your sins. One of the few things that change for the better as I get older is the fact that I can't commit nearly as many sins as I once did nor could I remember them if I did.

One of the times I did go to confession left me standing as the first person in line waiting for the priest to arrive to hear confessions. He was scheduled to arrive at 10:00 o'clock and I was the first in line.

Ten o'clock arrived and no priest. At ten fifteen there was still no priest. At ten-thirty we were still waiting. Along about ten forty-five he came rushing in and announced to me that he had been tangled up with some matter that he just couldn't leave and apologized for being so late.

I told him in response to the apology that I had brought myself to confession to confess my inability to deal with the sin of impatience and assumed that his late arrival was just a test. I don't know whether laughing in a confessional box is a sin but if it is, it was the priest doing the laughing, not me.

I pass this story along as I'm not sure where, when or if there is a statute of limitations that kicks in so that stupid things long since done are no longer held against us.

In my misspent youth, which lasted well into my thirties, I found myself in a situation where I had consumed a few "pops" and was feeling quite relaxed. I walked into the locker room to use the washroom and there hanging on the wall in the washroom was that famous Karsh photograph of Winston Churchill.

I always admired Winston Churchill and believed, as did many others, that it was his spirit as much as anything else that led to the Allied success in World War II. I felt that hanging his photograph in a washroom was totally inappropriate and an insult to the grand old fellow.

In my mind, such as it was at that moment, the picture of the man who was instrumental in freeing Europe should also be freed from it's present demeaning location.

Not freed. In the spirit of the man himself, it should be Liberated and I was the man to see to it.

The following morning, I was a little late getting up, I was greeted by Wanda with the words, "What on earth is that picture doing sitting in our living room?"

I tried to explain that it was a matter of respect and that the photo has now found a better home than it had late last night.

"Take it back" she ordered.

"I can't take it back" I told her.

"If I do it will probably wind up in the same awful location where I found it and I will probably get tossed out of the club on my ear, or worse."

I was confident that had I not been providing a major part of the bar revenue for the club I would have been tossed out some time ago.

"We'll find a nice place and hang it here" I offered.

""You can't hang it here" she told me. "We have people come in here from the club and they'll see it. You're still in nothing but trouble," she warned.

19

I had learned early in our relationship that when I was in a bit of a jam the best thing for me to do is suggest that Wanda could probably figure a way out of the mess. Now was such a time.

"You'll figure something out," I told her. "You're good at that sort of stuff." It sounded a little bit like that great line in Butch Cassidy and the Sundance Kid when they were in a mess and Sundance said, "Keep thinking Butch. That's what you're good at."

At any rate, when I got home from work that night Wanda was working on some needlepoint and the picture was nowhere in sight.

"Where's Winston?" I asked.

She pointed to the needlework. There under a beautiful vase of Marigolds that was being needle-pointed into place, was Winston S. Churchill, the man of the century.

That needle-point hangs in a quiet and respectful part of our home. More often than not it goes unnoticed. For those who may stop and look at it if you sense the words being spoken "Never before has so much been owed by so many to so few", it isn't the Marigolds speaking. It's a man who appreciates Liberation.

Who is She?

Wanda was born in Atholville, New Brunswick, a small town outside Campellton. She was one of four having an elder brother and two younger sisters.

Her mother was French-Catholic. Her father was English-Protestant. In those days that was very important, especially in small towns like Atholville. Father disappeared from their lives when she was a very young girl.

A kid's life in Atholville consisted of sliding down the hilly streets without worrying about traffic, ice skating on rivers and ponds and occasionally putting enough change together to pay for an hour or two of indoor skating and revelling in the fact that your toes weren't freezing from the cold.

School started in September and went on through June. She claims to have never gone to school in anything other than wool as it was always cold. That may be true. When we watch the weather channel it seems that part of the country spends a lot of time under a lot of snow.

On the other hand, Paine Stewart the golfer when commenting on Ireland was reported to have said, "I love the place. It's never dark. It was light when I went into the pub and it was light when I came out. I love the place." A lot depends on what you want to remember.

School was a delight. That's why it hurt so much when her mother had to tell her that she had to quit and get a job to help support the family. Brother Jim, had already left school and moved to Hamilton where he could find work and find a place for his mother and three sisters. Like so many other Maritimers, they headed down the road to find work in Ontario. Now we advise our children to stay in school. Get the education you need to survive. There once was a time when that wasn't an option and education came from living life. Wanda and I both got much of our education in that way.

While the family lived in New Brunswick they were considered poor, even by New Brunswick standards. The kids never knew they were poor. They knew about school and skating, shovelling snow to earn a quarter, picking berries and walking over rocks to dip their feet in cold streams. They knew they had to look after their siblings. They knew that Mom would have a nice meal ready when they came home at the end of the day. They learned to love home-made soup and stews and meat pies made from the most inexpensive cuts you could find.

As they had several relatives who were fishermen the meal often consisted of their catch of the day. As some were lobster fishermen the meal, quite often on weekends, consisted of lobsters that found their way onto the kitchen table. While the world complained about the price of lobsters, Wanda and family were often answering the question, "Would you like another one?" by saying "Sure. Why not. We've got lots."

When Jim, who had bought an old used car, was driving the family to their newly rented house in Hamilton, they stopped and ate their lunch at the old picnic tables that once dotted our highways. They laugh now when they think of sitting on the side of the road watching the traffic and eating the preserve jars of lobsters that an aunt had given them to have for lunch on their trip. There they were, poor as church mice. Waving to the passing cars and eating lobster, then going down the road.

Hamilton brought new friends. A job at a bank and a family attitude that somehow affirmed that when there is a problem everyone pitches in to try to make it right.

We met at a dance where I didn't want to be and where she made it clear that if I wanted to drive her home I had to give her brother a ride as well. Of course I agreed.

Three children, a successful Real Estate career for her, you can see the Masters Sales Award hanging prominently on our wall, a great golf swing and a terrific life later I can still make her laugh.

She still works hard at making sure I wear socks that match and that the buttons on my jacket are properly aligned.

I sometimes try to tell her how absolutely fortunate it has been for her that I happened to attend at the dance where we met. She reminds me of the story told about Ed Schreyer who was the Premier of Manitoba and also served as Canada's Governor General.

It seems that Mr. Schreyer and his wife decided to take a driving holiday through some of the back roads of Manitoba. They stopped for gas in a little town and the attendant recognized Mrs. Schreyer as a person he knew and dated in High School.

After they drove off Mr. Schreyer said, "Life and its twists and turns is amazing. Here you are driving with the former Premier of Manitoba having served as the Governor General of Canada when you could have married that fellow who wound up as a gas attendant."

Mrs. Schreyer responded, "If I had married him instead of you, I would have still wound up being married to the former Premier of Manitoba and Governor General of Canada."

I wonder what Ed might have wound up doing. Quite possibly pumping gas in a small town in Manitoba. Quite probably, according to Mrs. Schreyer.

Thursday Afternoons

Wanda always worked at staying trim and vowed never to have the need to increase her dress size beyond a ten. She fusses about it. I still see her as the girl I met at the dance.

We all have that time in our lives when we know we can eat whatever we wish and eat as much as is served. We then work it off so that within a day it's no longer noticeable.

She brags of going through the pre-natal checks while carrying Tammara, our first daughter, and going through the check-up and finding that she had only gained a pound since the last visit. Her response to that piece of knowledge would be to drive to the Stoney Creek Dairy and order their super-duper banana split with three scoops of ice cream, three separate toppings, whipped cream, sprinkles and a cherry. She knew she would be rid of the effects of that raid long before her next scheduled pre-natal visit. She was right.

Be careful with the eating. Be a non-smoker. Drink a social wine occasionally and do none of those things while you are pregnant. Exercise. Take Tai Chi classes. Look after yourself. She always does.

Suddenly, you find yourself in a waiting room with other ladies waiting for your turn to be re-examined. You wonder why there are so many other ladies in the waiting room. You learn that Thursdays are "call back days".

You learn that your mammogram showed a small growth and should be re-checked. You learn that the tests results will be sent to your family physician within a few days and you're advised to make an appointment to review the results.

You explain that your family physician is away until the end of next week. You're advised to see him as soon as possible and are informed that the results will be sent out before that time. You feel just a little bit better when the nurse informs you that you have a very small tumour but very often such growths are found to be benign.

You confirm again, that the results will be in the hands of your physician as soon as he returns, a week from Monday. You walk through the waiting room and are astounded at how many ladies have been called back to just one clinic of many.

We take each other by the hand and we sit quietly in the car for a few minutes. Both tear up. Both wonder how long it will take to get from this Thursday until a week from Monday so that you can see some test results. It already feels like a month. We both tear up. We both realize that no matter what the results may show, the world has just changed for us.

A Tall Man and a Little Girl

Neither of us have really liked crowds. We learned many years ago that the shoulder seasons, early Spring and late Autumn, were good times to schedule vacations rather than battle the high season crowds.

I am a bit of an American Civil War buff so we have often traveled down through Pennsylvania, on into Virginia and the Carolinas. They are about five or six weeks ahead of us in the Spring and Fall hangs on for those same extra five or six weeks. It's a great time to play golf and it's a nice time to spend touring.

After six visits to Gettysburg Wanda will no longer allow me to stop there because she has seen enough. As she has put it so succinctly, "people may see ghosts in Gettysburg but they're not going to see me." No more stops at that Civil War site.

That still hasn't stopped me from sneaking into Bull Run, Harpers Ferry, Petersburg or Appomattox where the Civil War ended with General Lee surrendering to General Grant. I just can't turn off the by-pass at Gettysburg anymore.

One of our Fall trips had taken us to Cape Cod while John Kennedy was still President. We drove to his house at Hyannis Port which, for security reasons, was surrounded by a very high solid wooden fence. We stopped at the security barricade at the end of that street but were unable to see anything. We were very shortly joined by a security officer asking why we were there. We explained we were down from Canada, we admired the President and wanted to see his home. The officer confirmed the Ontario license plate and, remember this is very much pre-terrorist times, suggested, "If I were you and wanted a picture of the house, I would wait until the security officer was not at this barricade and I would stand up on the bumper of my car, hold the camera over my head, point it in the house direction and snap the picture. Now, if I saw you doing that, you could be in trouble."

He then went on to tell me that he had to take a walk down to his other post position and that I had best not be here when he came back. We shook hands. He left. I got up on the bumper, pointed the camera and got some great pictures. Now in today's world that might very well get me shot or at least get me a term in Gitmo. Then it was just a case of good people each acting sensibly.

The encounter did leave us both with a good feeling about the Boston, Cape Cod, New England area. We have made several visits and included a great visit to the shrine of all of us members of the Red Sox Nation, Fenway Park. That was fun.

We had never driven through the New England States that touched the Atlantic. We decided one Fall that was the trip. We followed a late Fall hurricane that had just buzzed the area and made our way up the coast.

After many years of training from our resident Maritimer I had learned to clean up a lobster in quick time so I was even able to keep up reasonably well with Wanda. The seafood was great. The Fall colours were great. We found a Donald Ross designed golf course that was built in the 1930s and it was great. We had no itinerary and were just poking our way up the coast towards St. Andrews New Brunswick.

We were close to the town of Kennebunkport Maine which is the home of the Bush family. George Bush, the father, is known as forty-one as he was the 41st President. George W. is known as forty-three.

Contrary to what we might have heard, the New Englanders we met were extremely pleasant and open and surprisingly aware of Canada. To New Englanders we are not just a great white blob at the top of their weather map.

They boasted of the openness of the town visits made by Bush forty-one and were proud of the fact that Bill Clinton often visited with forty-one and the two spent time together and appeared to be good friends. We were very courteously directed to the Bush residence that sits on the far edge of town right on the Atlantic.

The lady that directed us to their house operated a stationery store right next to a very attractive little restaurant that, apparently, is frequented by Bush forty-one. She was so pleasant that we decided to stop on the way back, say thanks and buy something. We chatted. We asked about him and she told us how surprised she was when she realized George forty-one was so tall and told us the following story about him.

He and Barbara had pulled up to the front of the restaurant for dinner. They were surrounded by the usual group of Secret Service people and Security personnel. As forty-one was moving away from the car a very little girl, aged three or four, walked through the phalanx of guards, walked right up to the President and proceeded to tell him that she had just had a terrific day and wanted to tell someone about it. She and her Mom had gone to the beach. They bought ice cream. They went out on a boat and they saw some people digging out clams. She took off her shoes and walked right in the ocean. She just knew that George 41 wanted to know about her great day. She had to pick someone.

All of this took place while the Secret Service and other people were busy checking the rooftops and surrounding windows for threats to the President. Our story teller said she never realized how tall forty-one was until she watched this very tall man leaning over this very little girl and hanging on her every word as she told about her day. It was clearly a great day for a little girl. It was obviously a good day for forty-one as well.

And what the heck, anybody that likes baseball as much as forty-one can't be all bad.

Deflections

If you want to make absolutely certain that you will not think about something all you need to do is set your mind to not think about that thing. Suddenly, you find it impossible to think about almost anything else.

Try it.

Tell yourself you will not think about a yellow bird and see what pops into your mind and stays there. I remember walking past a friend and humming a few bars of that stupid old song, "I'm a Lumberjack but that's okay." Several weeks later he walked over to me and said," Every time I see you I start humming, 'I'm a Lumberjack but that's okay.' Shame on you for putting that in my head", he said.

Now, please don't get upset with me if you start carrying a stupid old song around in your head.

When you're told on a Thursday to make an appointment with your physician for a week and a half later to discuss a medical test report, it's very difficult to get that out of your head. You try not to worry about it. You try not to wonder. You can't talk to anyone about it except each other as it may not be a problem. Why concern anyone else?

You go out for dinner three times in the same week but you don't eat all that much. You go out for lunch during the week, which is something you very seldom do. You play a couple of games of golf but you don't play very well and you don't care much about your score. You turn down an invitation to a barbeque. You read the paper but you don't really care about the news. You check to see how large two centimetres really might be. You find yourself looking at the same page of the book you're reading and then realize that you have been looking at that same page for the past thirty minutes and you still don't know what it says.

You look at each other when you think you're not being seen. You touch each other on the shoulder when you pass in the kitchen. You wonder how much longer it is until your appointment next Monday and you wonder why it takes so long for a day to pass.

You try not to think about the news that you might get next week. You try not to let your eyes moisten and try even harder to not let it show. You fail.

You think of another reason to drive to the store.

Pay Attention

I mentioned earlier that Wanda and I met at a dance where I really didn't want to be. My friend Ted, who I knew since grade six, actually introduced us. It was an introduction that I wasn't about to forget.

I learned at an early stage to listen carefully when people were being introduced and to make a special effort to remember their name and to call them by name as soon as possible to reinforce the introduction information.

I learned that this was a smart thing to do. Unfortunately, all too often I didn't do that and would wind up a few minutes later having no idea of the name of the person to whom I was speaking.

One of my more memorable gaffes came when I was introduced to two persons at the golf club and invited to join them for a game. The introductions were made and we teed off. As we were walking off the tee I said to the one person I was sure that I had the name, "Excuse me but what is the other fellow's name? I missed it but I think its Jim."

"I missed it too", he admitted, "But I think your right. It's Jim."

I suggested that we call him Jim a couple of times and see what happens. If he reacts then we know we were correct. If we're wrong, he'll correct us.

For the next four hours we very comfortably settled in to having our friend respond when we were saying, "Nice shot Jim or this is your ball here Jim" or asking Jim what his score was for the card.

It was an enjoyable afternoon and we agreed to put in some patio time and have a "pop" before we left for the day.

One of the members walked by, waved at our table and said "Hi, Dave. How are you doing?"

"Who the hell is Dave?" I asked.

"That's me", said our new friend. It seems he was just too nice a guy to correct the two louts that had just spent four hours calling him by the wrong name.

A good friend of mine enjoyed the story but topped it by telling of the time he was at a fancy dinner banquet and was seated at a table for eight. Introductions were made all around and people identified themselves and the company that they represented.

There was much two handed hand shakes and sincere looking in the eye and plenty of the old "glad to meet you" going on. My friend had, of course, clearly identified himself and his firm.

After dinner and after the speeches were over the persons at the table did some socializing and more glad handing. I think it's now called networking, by those who now consider themselves consultants. One of the gentlemen turned to my friend and asked, "What Company did you say you are connected with?"

My friend told him.

"Oh", said the dinner companion.

"Is there any chance you would know so and so?" asking about the man himself.

"I know him quite well," answered my friend. "In fact I sometimes sleep with his wife."

The moral of the story is, listen and listen well.

Especially when introductions are being made.

The Real Estate Lady

In 1984 I was in the construction business. Dan was working with me. Tammara was just finished University and Linda was still living at home.

The Canadian Banks, in their wisdom, seemed to have followed a policy of lending money to every country in the world at interest rates in the fifteen to eighteen percent range. This meant that the Banks felt they could lend to Canadian businesses with interest in the twenty-two to twenty-four percent range or not lend at all.

When many of the bad foreign loans went into default the Banks responded to their foreign lending mistakes by tightening credit on Canadian businesses while waiting for the Government to bail them out of their bad decisions with tax-payer dollars.

The strategy worked well for the Banks but the treatment of Canadian borrowers caused a huge rush of mortgage foreclosures and business failures. Sound familiar?

We went out of business, not because we had over-borrowed, but because we could no longer pay the twenty-four percent interest demanded by the Banks. We started over at age forty-eight after the Bank seized the business and our home and sold them for a quarter of their value.

We lived at a time when it was considered to be quite okay to be a stay at home mother. It wasn't the Father Knows Best television show attitude where father went off to work at some mysterious job and mother stayed at home and baked cookies while wearing a fancy dress with ruffles, but it was somewhat close. The era of the career woman had not yet dawned.

We were married in 1957 so in 1984 Wanda had been the driving force in our home for twenty-seven years and had held down all those jobs and carried all the responsibility that came from raising three children and keeping a husband straightened out.

When the Banks had finished doing their number on us we moved into a rental house and tried to figure out what one does next when you have just been cleaned out, no one holds a job and everyone has been used up trying to meet unreachable obligations.

Wanda decided it was time to become the Real Estate Lady. Determination. You bet. The exams were passed. An office connection was made and a career was launched. Ten years later a limousine picked her up at the doorstep and drove her to the awards dinner where she picked up the plaque that recognized her as one of the top producers in the company.

In the meantime we had launched our own business with some success and with the knowledge and comfort that Wanda had given us the space needed to survive. It also bought her a golf membership and a determination to best a new game.

Although she had enjoyed skiing and had enjoyed tennis, had tried horseback riding and declared that effort to be a game for fools, she had never hit a golf ball.

She started on the short course and spent every spare minute learning one of the most frustrating games in the world. She agreed to take a golf trip to courses that proved to be too difficult but came home determined to go back when she could play better and did. Eventually, golf trips became one of the best parts of our vacation plans and took us to some of the best scenery and interesting places in the country.

She was the one in the family that made the hole in one. I could only watch when the two gentlemen who had been assigned to play with us that day hugged and kissed her. I took a five on the same hole.

She was the one who was playing with her brother-in-law in Florida and was paired with two other gentlemen. The following day I was with the brother-in-law and her when I heard the two men that had played with them the day before yell over to our fairway, "Hey Paul, is Wanda whupping yer fanny agin today?" There was no need to answer.

All this took place while she was quietly but effectively finding the right house in the right location for people who enjoyed doing business with her.

I came home one warm summer day and she was sitting on the deck sipping on a lemonade.

"I made a decision today," she said.

"What's that all about," I asked.

"I've retired from real estate," she replied. "and it's all the fault of golf."

"What happened?"

"Well, I went over to the club this morning and played eighteen with a couple of my friends and we stayed for lunch. It was just gorgeous. I played well. The temperature was perfect. There was no wind and lunch was great."

"Then I thought to myself, why on earth should I walk away from this kind of day in order to rush through a shower in order to race to the office, pick up material and go and sit in someone's non air conditioned house on the off chance that someone else might want to come along and buy it?"

"No reason I can think of," I answered.

"Me neither", she said. "So I retired."

Sounds like a good plan to me.

The Doctor is In

We made the appointment the previous week so that we could meet with the Family Doctor as soon as he returned from vacation. The appointment was set for ten o'clock.

Wanda called at nine to make sure the test reports had been received. They had not and Wanda was advised to re-schedule the appointment. She called me to tell me of the situation. I had gone to the office first thing in the morning. If you wonder why I would have done that you can re-read my comments on Deflections.

She told me she had already called the screening clinic and they assured her they were faxing the report to the Doctor immediately. I told her I would contact the Doctor and one way or another, we would get an appointment today.

The Doctor's office was helpful and we were to be "squeezed in" at four o'clock. We arrived at three-thirty only to be told that the Doctor had not had an opportunity to read the report and that we should re-schedule.

There was a slight escalation and we suggested that we would read the report alongside the Doctor if necessary but we would meet today.

It's a very helpful and cooperative office and they do their very best. However it's well to know that the dictionary defines anxiety as being "the state of being anxious". It goes on to define anxious as "being worried and tense".

As we met and the Doctor read the report, Wanda and I held hands. We don't do that all that often but there comes a time when hands should be held.

"Well" said the Doctor, "according to the report, you have cancer."

The words just take on a particular thud.

"Why are you tearing up?" he asked.

"Because you just told me I had cancer" with a broken voice.

"It's small. It's treatable. We'll arrange a meeting with an extremely qualified surgeon and we'll get started quickly. We'll have you scheduled for surgery within two weeks. We're starting on a journey together." That was said very kindly.

"Are you sure?" asked Wanda.

"We're sure. You have cancer," he replied.

"No", I said. "Wanda has to carry the pail but we have cancer."

A Journey

The Doctor told us we were about to start on a journey. There are journeys and there are journeys. We knew this one would have no maps, no GPS, no charts to mark shoals and no harbours that could be considered safe. It was, however, good terminology.

It started with a drive home in silence.

When we got home I suggested that Wanda take a lie down and I told her we would need to tell the kids. We've often observed that no matter the age, if you have children, you will always be a mother and father. You need, somewhere along the way, to stop being a parent but you never stop being a mother or father. There is no way that calls such as I was about make, can ever be easy.

Three calls. Three times I had to say in various ways, "We had a Doctor's appointment today and we were told that your mother has cancer. We'll tell you more when we know more."

Dan was tough to talk to because he was also dealing with the fact that his wife, Vickie, is already carrying the load that her mother is a cancer patient. They were already carrying heavy stuff.

Linda cried.

Tammara, asked, "Are you okay?" I said, "no."

Then you wait for a call that sets an appointment with a surgeon and a surgery date. That comes in two or three days and the surgery date is set for two or three weeks later. It's only when you get off the phone that you realize the surgery date is Wanda's birthday.

Happy Birthday, Hon.

There is no one correct way to handle these situations. Some take it as a load they need to carry by themselves. Others go into denial. Others want and need the support of their friends. There is no one correct way to handle these situations. Wanda and I agreed that we need to tell the immediate family and that we should send some kind of message to our closest friends that let them know that, for a while at least, our life has changed. We need to learn as much as we can about the disease and the treatments so you poke for information and worry about finding out things that you don't want to find out about. There was that flurry of phone calls and e-mails that informed most of our closest friends. I'm sure this kind of feeling, in one way or another, hits everyone when they get this kind of news.

Wanda has always had a large circle of friends. Good news takes forever to get out but bad news spreads quickly. She started to get cards. Flowers arrived at the door. Home baked muffins came with a knock at the door and handed in without any words being spoken. Offers of help came from everywhere. Offers of "nice" just arrive.

People we hardly knew, some of them cancer survivors, called and offered to just talk about their experiences and, by their just being there, passed on the encouraging news that it's a fight, it is a journey, but it is something that can be beaten.

We learned of so many people who have carried the same burden or who have helped someone else in their life to carry such a load. They wanted to talk about it. They wanted to help and I suppose, in some ways they wanted to be helped or to have their fight vindicated.

Kindness and encouragement can be over-whelming. You learn again, or sometimes for the first time, that in a world that is too often ugly and mean that there are wonderful people out there. Many of them have troubles that reach way beyond your own. You try hard to keep that in mind.

Then sometimes when it's quiet or you're trying to get back to sleep, your own situation and your own journey problems hit hard. You cry but you first put a pillow over your face or go to another part of the house where you can't be heard. Sometimes a feeling of sadness washes over you like a giant wave and you lose it. I truly believe that's okay.

The next morning you see each other. You hug and wish each other a good morning. You hope you weren't heard the night before. You know you were and that too hurts.

The surgery day arrives and you are at your instructed department at seven-thirty in the morning. The people at McMaster Hospital are terrific. They take the required x-rays and blood tests. They inject some mysterious dye and some radioactive tracing material. Then you wait with your husband and your daughter until the afternoon when you are wheeled into the O.R. They check your name on your tag and they ask a personal question, just to make sure they have the right person. They ask for your birth date. It's today. Happy Birthday Hon.

The procedure takes about two hours. For those who are waiting it only seems like six hours. They sit in the cafeteria trying not to think about what is going on elsewhere in the hospital and trying to hang on to this thing called composure. You're not fully successful.

Finally, the clock tells you that it's time to go to the recovery area where you will meet with the surgeon and wait out the time needed before you take the patient home. The surgeon arrives and tells you that she is confident that she was successful in removing the tumour and that it appears there was no further invasion by the cancer but that no one can be sure until they get a pathology report. You thank her and you thank her and you thank her. You arrange a follow-up meeting for two weeks later.

You get the lady home. You feed her some soup. She drifts off for the night and wakes up the next morning "feeling sore but pretty good".

Over the next few days some of your friends call and you assure them that all went well and "you're feeling pretty good".

You arrive at the surgeon follow-up meeting early. She seems a little annoyed.

She tells you that the pathology report indicates that there was some evidence of invasion of some lymph nodes and that there were some cells in the margins area of the surgery that should be cleaned out.

Thud.

After some discussion you agree that you should meet with the radiation oncologist and get some additional input before you make a decision on a second surgery. An early appointment is made.

The radiation oncologist is very confident in what he does and tells us that an additional surgery will not only remove some of the bad stuff that may be located but it will give them a better fix on where and how to attack difficult areas with radiation. The decision to have such work done, however, rests with the patient.

"When would radiation start?" Wanda asked.

"Three or four weeks after you completed your chemotherapy", he answered.

Thud.

"No one talked about the need for chemo", one or the other of us offered. "Where did this come from and what does that do for us?"

A short while later we found ourselves meeting with a medical oncologist and learning the facts and percentages of success when each or any of the ongoing procedures are followed. The decision was made to repeat surgery and to go into a radiation treatment program. These decisions are so personal that no one can possibly comfortably advise another person. The radiation oncologist kept reassuring us with facts and percentages that with treatment the chances are strong that Wanda should live, in his words, "A long and happy life." You need to believe. You want so much to believe.

In the meantime some wonderful things were happening in our lives. The fresh bread and dinner invitations continued to arrive. The neighbour, in the true sense of the word, called and invited Wanda to just go for a walk with her so that she could explain what she went through and how she dealt with the same disease. The lady at the golf club that had a very serious bout with the same disease several years ago suggested lunch so that she could tell her story and hear Wanda's. The friend that had been recently diagnosed wanted to meet and share feelings and stories. The close friends called almost every day "just to touch base".

You try to reciprocate. Not because anyone was keeping books or trying to stay even with invitations or time but because you recognize there is a circle of friends and people who care and you want to strengthen the circle if you can. You want and need your friends.

You also come to recognize that, sadly, the disease runs rampant. It is an epidemic. It is a pandemic. When stricken with it yourself you come to learn how many others are fighting the same fight or have fought the fight. You tell your friends. You tell your daughters. Get screened. Get tested by any means available. Throw the cigarettes away. Take care. Don't take this journey if there is any way to avoid it.

It was second surgery day. Wanda was checked in by ten o'clock and surgery was scheduled for two. Linda was there at noon and as she was saying good bye and wishing her mother good luck as she was taken into the O.R., Wanda said to her, "See that your Dad gets something to eat. He hasn't eaten anything all day."

The procedure was expected to take approximately two hours. Linda and I sat in the cafeteria watching the world go by and watching the clock not move.

I'm Irish and I'm Catholic. This doesn't mean I believe in everything that either of those things presents or stereotypically represents. As a person with Irish background I kind of believe in the "little people". For those of you who don't know about the little people they are never seen but they do things or they may plant ideas or even may nudge people in a direction they suggest we follow. Bert, in our office, believes that if you can't find something it's usually because the little people have taken it because they need it and they will return it when they're finished. She says they don't always return it to the same place and that's why, sometimes, you find it in a place where you least expect it to be. Catholics and others believe in angels and that they can sometimes do the same job. Either way, whether it's the little people or the angels or some other mysterious force, it can't hurt to have them on your side. If you believe that this stuff is merely an opiate, that's okay too. Sometime an opiate makes sense.

McMaster is a teaching hospital. It is also very renowned as a children's hospital. The people of the City of Hamilton raise millions of dollars to support the children's hospital endeavours. It's becoming internationally famous.

As we sat in the cafeteria area waiting for two hours to pass I couldn't help but see the number of little tots who were in the hospital for various reasons. Many of them were there for surgery. They would walk along, carrying their Teddy Bears or favourite toy, wearing bathrobes that had bunnies or squirrels or happy faces on them, holding the hands of Mom or Dad or sometimes Gramma or Grampa. They would be pointing or asking questions or seeing things they had never seen before and listening intently to the answers given by their hand-holder. It was a time of complete trust. It was written all over their little faces. The concern and the pain was written in the faces of the hand-holder.

I was watching this picture while keeping one eye on the clock that wouldn't move and I said to Linda, "I can't believe that anyone in a position of trust could hurt these little kids. I think I have enough time to go find the kind of person that won't stand up against that kind of scum and punch them in the nose." I felt that would make me feel better.

"Don't do that Dad," she said. "We've got enough trouble at the moment."

I took her advice. I guess it was just another deflection. Instead, I suggested that even though we are almost an hour before the procedure is expected to be finished we should take a walk. We did.

We walked along through the general section of the hospital and we came to a passageway that was marked "Private No Admittance".

Something nudged me to take a walk down that hallway. Linda and I were the only ones there.

Suddenly walking the towards us was Wanda's surgeon. She saw us and was smiling.

"What are you doing here?" I asked.

"I might ask the same thing of you," she said. "I'm here because the operation went so well that we were finished well ahead of schedule. I think we got what we needed. I think we're clear. We'll take the next step."

I thanked her and I thanked her and I thanked her.

I realized that it was only a coincidence that Linda and I and our surgeon all happened to be in exactly the same place, where none of us should have been, at a time when none of us should have been there.

Coincidences happen. Besides, there is no such thing as "little people" or angels that nudge things along or should cause you to feel good that they might be on your side. If I believed that sort of stuff I would have recognized that this was indeed little bit more than a strange coincidence.

Two weeks later a pathology report noted that the area was clear, the hormone therapy was well started and the radiation treatment should start within twelve weeks to be most effective.

It is indeed a Journey.

The Door Stop

Someone told me that the obsession with the disease will fade as it does with most problems, to some degree or other. I know that's true because many of our friends and relatives have struggled with incredible problems and have coped and often totally overcome. At this point it is still the first thing I think of in the morning and the last thing I think of before I go to sleep.

Wanda had recently gone through a surgery and was taking care of some complications before the next step could be taken. It was a difficult wait made more difficult because the next treatment step had to be taken within a certain time frame in order to be most effective. Again, time has very different speeds at different times. In this case every day that was used up dealing with a complication was one day less on the treatment efficiency scale. It's hard not to obsess. Those days passed quickly and the deadline became more and more frightening.

Then one day, out of the blue, something happens or something is heard and you find yourself laughing. There hasn't been much laughing in the last while, it seemed to have disappeared along with whistling and humming so it comes as a bit of a surprise.

I'm in the financial planning business and constantly meet with clients. During one such meeting the client and I agreed that the banks continually nickel and dime clients with charges. Much of the time we don't notice, don't care and in some cases despair at ever increasing charges. Cable TV people have learned the same skill.

My client and friend commented on the fact that he recently received notice from his bank that his fees for his safety deposit box were about to triple. He told me he was annoyed enough to cancel the safety deposit box and empty it.

"What did you keep in the box?" I asked.

"Well we had the usual important papers things. A couple of insurance policies, the house deed, Will copies, some stuff I invested in years ago, that sort of thing."

"What sort of thing had you invested in that you would keep in a safety deposit box?" I asked.

"Some guy told me years ago that I should invest in silver. I didn't know anything about it so I took his suggestion and bought a bar of silver and put it in the box. It has been there ever since."

"Okay," say I, "but now you've had a fight with your banker and moved on. What did you do with the bar of silver?"

"I took it home. I painted it black and I use it for a door stop. I've probably got the only $5,000 door stop in the country."

I laughed. It really felt good.

If there is a lesson to be learned from this episode it isn't about anxiety or obsession with a problem. The lesson that I could see should be directed at those persons who break into other's houses and steal.

Don't just take the rings and the flat screen television. Take the door stop.

I Could Never Make a Living At It

Golf is a really dumb game. It's also an impossible game to play and that's probably why millions of people, world wide, play at it. Someone, somewhere, will tell you that it's fun. What could make more sense or cause you to have more fun than to take a tiny white ball and to take a crooked stick with the object of the game being to hit the tiny ball with the crooked stick into a tiny hole that is four to five hundred yards away and to do that with no more than four or five hits. If you find that to be too easy to accomplish you can play on a golf course loaded with trees, ponds and areas full of sand called sand traps. If you take more than four or five hits you may start to feel more than a little frustrated but there is always someone around to tell you that you had best relax and enjoy the day.

Doctors have been known to advise patients who have high blood pressure to take up the game if they don't already play or to give up the game if they do already play.

In my case, I was introduced to the game by my two older brothers-in-law. No one had any money to put towards the playing of the game at that time of our lives. We learned, however, that if we got to a particular course early enough we could sneak on at the second hole and get off the course before we got to the last hole in order to avoid Security. I may have played the game for five years before I realized that a golf course has eighteen holes, not the sixteen that we played early on Saturdays.

We all started with the cheapest golf clubs we could buy and many of us bought one set of clubs and split them with a friend so that one person played with all the even numbered clubs and the other used the clubs with odd numbers.

Golf balls were also a premium item. Most golf was played with balls that we found. We never considered them to be a "lost ball". They were "experienced" balls and were expected to change directions when we yelled at them to stay out of the water or to get out of the sand. The least expensive golf balls around at that time were sold through a drug store chain long since gone. The Tamblyn golf balls cost something like three for a dollar. They were round. They were white. They were new. They were never used on a shot that might be lost in the water or in the woods until they had gained considerable experience. They were just too valuable.

Sometime ago Wanda and I were playing with some friends in Florida on a course that ran alongside a swamp area seriously infested with snakes and home to an occasional alligator. My friend hit a shot that drifted into the swamp.

His wife said, "You're not going in there to try to retrieve that are you?"

"Not unless you heard someplace this morning that they've stopped making golf balls," he replied. There is a smart man.

I joined an excellent golf club when I was twenty-seven years old. I couldn't afford to join but we stretched payments out and I played golf while Wanda, who did not play at that time, enjoyed the social aspects of the place. We've made friends there that we have had for more than forty years. We've made friends last year.

We joined the Golf Club and considered the dues our cottage costs or our summer vacation. For the most part, it has been fun and when Wanda took up the game it became even more fun.

As I was never well skilled at the game I couldn't teach her much other than to play at a quick pace and to not talk when someone is hitting a shot. The end result is that she has become a good recreational golfer and has a lot of fun most days.

Every golfer in the world seems to feel that they are accredited golf instructors and will immediately start to give instructions or helpful "hints" to every other golfer within earshot. Everyone likes to give the instructions but hardly anyone likes to hear them.

I often played with the same three men and the four ladies sometimes played together. We decided it would be good to have the eight of us play one day and then to go to someone's place after the game, have a couple of pops, eat some barbeque and tell some lies.

We agreed that two men would play with two ladies in the same group but that no two spouses would play together. After the game was finished, Marsha said, "That was terrific. That is the first time I played when I took a hundred shots and didn't get a hundred lessons."

Her husband Gord allowed as he was just trying to help.

Golfers, as with any other group, break down into various categories:

Golfers who play every shot where it lies and who play every ball all the way into the hole.

Golfers who play for nickels, or more, and who circle every putt for five minutes and then miss it by a foot.

Golfers who don't play for nickels or more and who circle each putt for five minutes and then miss it by a foot.

Golfers who defend the traditions of golf and who demand that ties be worn in the clubhouse and that a special lounge be maintained for men only because golf traditions must be maintained. They then take their NASA developed golf clubs with club heads the size of a Buick and take to the course using golf balls made of materials discovered in mysterious laboratories that assist in having the ball travel an extra hundred yards no matter how weird the swing, jump into their power carts, set their range finders and GPS technology and declare once more that the traditions of golf must be maintained as they open a beer and head down the first fairway. We've got a lot of those and more coming.

Golfers who go out with their friends, whack the ball around, may or may not bother keeping scores and who have a nice day.

It took me a long time to learn to be one of the last group but it's a good way to play provided you are not trying to play with one of the other types. Golfers will make each other crazy if they get playing with a different category of player.

It may be just pretend golf to the purist but we play to a different set of rules. I've listed a few:

If a ball ends up behind a tree and you cannot move the tree you may move the ball so as to protect the environment.

If a ball goes into the water and you didn't intend to have that happen you may hit another ball without penalty.

If a ball is putted over the hole and does not drop into the hole the ball is considered to have dropped as the laws of gravity supersede the rules of golf.

If a shot does not work out the way you would have liked you are entitled to a do over or a Mulligan provided you do not delay play for those behind.

If you reach a score that is higher than you would have liked, or feel that you deserved, you may write the lower score on your scorecard provided that you add the proper number in the clubhouse before you submit your score to the handicap committee.

If you are confident that you can make your putt you may pick it up and declare a gimme. There is no limit to the length of a gimme provided you are playing with friends and not betting on the hole or the game.

Caveat - None of these rules may be used if you are playing in a competition or with people who do not have a reasonably good sense of humour.

There are some golf courses that have their own special rules that sometimes contribute to how you might enjoy the day. Wanda and I have often visited a small town in North Carolina and have played their local course that was reputedly designed by a legendary golf course designer.

On the entranceway door window leading to the pro shop there is a sign that says, "No guns allowed on the course." There is also a picture, for those who have trouble reading, of a revolver with a red bar through it.

"What is that all about?" Wanda asked when she first saw it.

"That, my dear" I responded knowingly, "Means that if someone down here wants to play through, we let them."

We occasionally play with Frank and Lois. They're fun to play with. They're both good players and neither get uptight when Wanda and I lapse into our "pretend golf" rules. We just go out and have some fun and buy each other a pop at the end of the day.

One day, we did not stop for that pop when the game was finished.

It was a gorgeous summer day. Part way through the game Frank let it be known that he was going in for some medical tests the following day. He said that he had been given a laxative to take in preparation for the tests and asked us to remind him to take the pill.

We were well into the game and with six holes to play I asked Frank when he was supposed to take his pill.

"I just took it. Lois reminded me."

As we played on Frank began to look more and more uncomfortable. He seemed to be getting more and more anxious to speed up play. He even gave himself a couple of "gimmes" that he would not have ordinarily have taken.

As we neared the clubhouse Frank announced that he would not be stopping for a drink following the game. He then announced that he was not going to finish the last hole but that he was going ahead because he wanted to get into the locker room quickly.

As he was set to speed off I said , "Frank, let me give you a piece of advice."

"What's that?" he asked.

"Please, never ever take a five hole laxative with six holes to play."

He made it in. He still speaks to me. He still reminds me about the day I gave him some really good advice.

It's a great game if you let it be. It's a game that has allowed us to be out on a beautiful day with our son Dan, Tammara, our grandchildren, ourselves. It's the only game that I know of where I can very occasionally make a shot that is just as good as a shot made by the best golfer in the world.

When the grandchildren, Kate and Adam were very small I used to take them over to the golf course and let them find golf balls. They would land back home with their pockets full and their clothes dirty. Vickie would pretend she was upset over the mess that grandpa brought home with him. Everyone knew better.

We were out in a wooded area late on a Sunday afternoon when we saw two people coming up the fairway in a cart. I told the grandkids to just stay in the woods and not make any noise until the couple in the cart moved through.

I recognized John and Betty. They were laughing and talking and kidding about the last shot. It just seemed right. John died, unexpectedly a while later but before his time.

I told Betty that story at a recent function. She said, "You've made me cry." I didn't mean to. It just looked so right that day.

Golf has taken us to so many great places and given us time with so many great people. David and Maureen are great people to golf with or travel to Carolina to chase golf balls or to sit on a back deck and listen to a veteran play taps at the end of a Carolina day.

Ted and Marianne braved being out on a golf course with an approaching electrical storm just so they could time getting Wanda and

I into the club house at the exact scheduled moment that our surprise fortieth wedding anniversary party was to start. Believe me, Ted wants no part of an electrical storm on a golf course or anywhere else.

Dan and I along with Ted and his son-in-law Scott took a trip to Hilton Head together to golf. On the first day out, sitting in a golf cart, Ted and I approached a home-owner that seemed to be trying to flip something over. We were curious.

"What are you doing?" we asked the guy with the long handled rake in his hands.

"I'm trying to flip this snake over," he replied. "If he has red spots on his belly he's very poisonous. No spots, no problems", he shrugged.

Ted and I both went straight in the air, landed standing up in the golf cart and left at flank speed. We're not sure which had the greater problem, the snake or the guy with the rake.

Wanda and I have played golf in Ireland, at Pinehurst and Pine Needles, in British Columbia and at Kananaska with the Rockies as a backdrop. In Florida, California, the desert where they advise you watch for scorpions and rattlers. On Donald Ross courses in Maine. One of us made a hole in one in Florida, it wasn't me. We followed the Alabama Golf Trail and checked out the history of the Civil Rights movement in Montgomery. We played overlooking the Bay of Fundy and ate the best seafood chowder ever at the Algonquin in New Brunswick then went to Prince Edward Island to make sure it was okay to golf and eat double lobster. It was. We've hit golf balls into a surreal mist in Charleston and then were delayed because there was an alligator in a sand trap on the second hole.

It has been great. It has been a great excuse to go somewhere and we have.

As we get along a golfer might measure years by referring to now being on the back nine. Some of the parts start to wear. I still sometimes hit a drive to the same area that I used to hit them thirty years ago. Not often. I realize that it's the work of the improved equipment and golf technology and not the result of any extra prowess of mine. It's more fun now, especially with my new rules listed earlier.

I had some knee surgery many years ago and was having problems with the other knee. I saw the same orthopaedic surgeon that I had seen many years ago and he informed me that the second knee was just worn down. I balked at his suggestion that a knee replacement might help.

I asked him if it would hurt the knee if I played golf without doing anything differently.

"Just move to the forward tees," he said. "After all, life is just a progression towards the forward tees."

How about that, I thought. I came to see a doctor and I get a philosopher.

The wife of a friend of ours decided to take up golf. As with so many tyros it's a tough game to learn. There aren't only the golf skills that need to be learned but there are also the rules and the etiquette.

Andy and his wife were put together with two strangers when they came to play a different course. Andy said that, as a golfer, she was horrible. On one hole, while the two strangers stood around watching this golf horror show unfold, she took six swings at a ball in a sand trap. Andy finally told her to just throw the ball out and on to the green. She did so and then accepted a hand out of the trap.

As she walked across the green she looked down and saw a coin that one of her most patient co-players had used as a ball marker.

"Look Andy", she said. "This must be my lucky day. I found a dime" and picked it up.

The strangers rolled their eyes. Andy announced, "Well I think we've had enough for today."

Wanda had a surgery scheduled for her birthday that fell on the following Monday. Sunday was a beautiful day. We decided to go over to the course at a quiet time, just the two of us, and play. I don't remember much of the game.

When we were playing the eighteenth hole I hit my shot reasonably close to the hole and put down a marker. Wanda chipped her shot even closer and then made her putt. I left my marker where I had placed it. I told her I wasn't going to putt.

"We'll be back. We'll finish this game another day", I said.

The minute we got clearance on a radiation schedule for Wanda we came home and booked two weeks away on a golf course in South Carolina. We've got a lot of games to play. We'll have fun doing it.

Just a Museum

The renowned jurist Oliver Wendel Holmes in speaking about the need for vacation once said, "I can do 52 weeks of work in 50 weeks but it's impossible to do 52 weeks of work in 52 weeks."

Justice Holmes, I'm sure, would be thrilled to know that I agree with him.

I've never been big on holidays primarily because I have enjoyed what I have done for a living for most of my working days. There are days when it's easy to hate your job with a passion but those have been more than offset with the pleasure that I've taken from my work, no matter what that work has been.

However, as time has moved along I have come to appreciate the time away from the every day grind and can settle into a break mode. There are times when I might even call such a break a holiday.

We have often taken such time away and spent it at a residential community with two golf courses on the property near a small town in North Carolina. We rent a house, play golf every other day, now that the old bones makes every day play a little tough, and we poke around looking for things that make small towns. We sometimes have friends or family come to stay and we play guide for them if they wish to see what might be around. We look forward to such visits because it makes us see things through the eyes of others and it helps us keep a sensible perspective on life. This is not always an easy thing to do when you are caught up in the maelstrom of every day stuff but it explains the Oliver Wendel Holmes observation.

When I sit out on the deck of our rental place I see a golf green close to our house and a beautiful picture of the twenty-five acre lake, two far off fairways and a feeder stream that grabs golf balls being hit towards the nearby green. It also provides a neat hiding refuge for the bird life that thrives. The darn things flutter and sing and stay very busy but seem to bring that restfulness that Justice Holmes sought and recognized.

The evenings are particularly enjoyable. I was sitting on the deck watching the trees melt into the darkness, just like the song McArthur Park says it does, single malt in hand, just winding down when I heard it.

Somewhere from the complex someone was smoothly playing a trumpet. Amazing Grace. It was played quietly and with a type of reverence one seldom hears in Church. Even the birds stopped and listened. The notes tailed off. There was a pause, then the unseen musician played Taps. In my mind I could see a flag being lowered as it should be, in sync with the sunset.

The following evening I made certain I was waiting on our deck to watch and listen as the sun went down. Walkers were passing by and I asked one of them if they knew anything about the person that played Amazing Grace and Taps at sundown.

"Oh sure", I was told. "That's old so and so. He's retired from the military. He's almost blind but he still participates in all our local shows. He has a great singing voice and every night at sundown he sits on his porch and plays those two pieces while his wife takes the flag down for the night. That's why we time our walk so that we're here. It helps take us out of the day".

I like telling stories. I like hearing stories. I like exchanging stories. Story telling is the passing of lore in such a way that cannot be duplicated by TV or passed along through e-mails or cell phone calls. It can be done through newspapers, to some degree, and through books to a greater degree. But who has time to read books in our busy important lives? Lore can best be preserved and passed along by people who have lived life and lived life experiences.

One of the greatest places to find such people is at lesser known museums where they spend time as volunteers. There is an extremely well done military museum in nearby Fayetteville that is the home of Fort Bragg and the training centre for airborne troops.

David and I decided to spend time to take in the museum while Maureen and Wanda did what they do very well. They went shopping. They are both Olympic class shoppers and possibly have their pictures on posters at the credit card companies with the over-write stating: "If you see these persons, be nice. They are working to save your job!"

While my friend wandered the museum checking out tanks, weapons, uniforms, letters and medals, I struck up a conversation with a volunteer who had landed in France on D-Day and had seen much of Europe through the eyes of an ordinary soldier. I told him stories I had heard. He told me stories he had lived. He was the museum.

It has been said that if you just stand in one place long enough the world will eventually all pass before you. While we talked and laughed and shook our heads at something stupid or something special, part of the world did pass by.

We watched an older gentleman climb up, with difficulty, on the museumed tank and point out the various controls and instruments that he used to operate the vehicle when he was in North Africa. His son seemed genuinely interested. Perhaps he was. Perhaps he was humouring an old man because he had heard all the stories many times. Either way, it was good to see.

We watched a younger man explain desert living conditions to his older parents. He had just done his tour in Iraq. He looked older than his years. Mom and Dad were just glad to see him home.

We watched a father and his uniformed son passing by. He was training to go. Dad just wanted to spend as much time with him as he possibly could. The young soldier looked like he was caught up in some great adventure. We've got to figure out how to stop doing this.

My friend the volunteer introduced me to another volunteer seated nearby. "I'm 91 years old" I was told. "I jumped into France on D-Day with the 82nd airborne. Fought in Korea. Got myself wounded. Did two tours in Viet Nam, and now I come here. Don't ever knock the 82nd airborne" he warned.

"Best outfit in the army. Every soldier worth his salt wants to be part of the 82nd. Knock the 82nd" he said, "and I'll take you down."

I just wanted to shake his hand. My volunteer friend said that he probably could "take me down". I agreed.

The day moved quickly. My friend the volunteer thanked me several times for visiting. I was there to thank him. It was a quiet drive back to our rental. We got there in time to sit out on the deck and listen to a fading veteran play Amazing Grace and Taps as the flag was lowered. It was quite a day.

I Never Noticed

We enjoyed our Fall and Spring breaks and tried to change destinations and routes so that we have come to see a lot of different places. Much of our traveling has been done by car because it's fairly easy to throw an extra jacket in the back seat or trunk or to add an extra few golf balls in a bag in case you run out. Most of the time these come back with added golf balls that we found on the trip.

When you are traveling by plane packing and weight becomes a much bigger problem. However, most of us take what we need and need what we take and we pay attention to the old adage that you should take half the clothing you think you need but take twice the money.

It becomes a little trickier when you are traveling north to south or south to north. You need the warmer stuff for north and the light stuff for south and you guess at what you might need in between.

We've travelled to a golf resort when it should have been warming for Spring and brought light clothing only to wind up putting on everything we owned to try to beat the cold.

"Coldest Spring we've had in forty years," we're told by the locals.

It bothers them a little but bothers us a whole lot more when we're paying a King's ransom for a room, pulling on a third pair of socks and watching the tulips fall over from last night's frost.

Our football game trip covered just about everything in the clothing and packing area. We needed walking around stuff because we were going to visit Scranton Pennsylvania where we knew we could find the Harry Houdini magician's Hall of Fame. We concluded that it was amazing that it hadn't disappeared years ago. We needed windbreakers for our visit to West Point. We needed football clothes and we needed golf clothes for the later part of our trip.

None of this really presented a problem because, as I said earlier, you just toss what you need in the back seat or trunk.

Tradition is very important at Military Colleges or places like West Point. We learned that all the statues of famous Generals that graduated from West Point face the parade ground with the exception of the statue of George Patton. His statue, at the request of his wife, faces the library not the parade grounds. Before approving the statue she demanded that it face the library because George claimed he could never find the place when he was a student.

We have a neighbour and friend who attended the Canadian Royal Military College in Kingston. Our friend is a very smart person and very successful businessman. He has served on major boards. He's a mover and a shaker in the true sense of the word and he and his wife, much to our delight, have become good friends with us. He has worked closely with a former Prime Minister of Canada. He was wise enough to marry a delightful lady who will telephone Wanda from holiday places just to see how she is doing. This man clearly knows what he is doing.

Yes, he did graduate with a degree from the Royal Military College.

Apparently, we were told by our friend, one of the traditions that goes with graduation from military college is to take a trip across Canada, with some fellow grads, before you report to your first official posting. If it wasn't a formal tradition perhaps it should become one.

The formal gear was shipped to their posting in Alberta and the new grads packed their duffel bags with necessities and set out to hitch hike their way to the Pacific Ocean then back to their base in Alberta. It was to be that one great unforgettable trip.

Day after day they slogged their way across Canada. They were on a mission.

I once had a British immigrant tell me that you could drive across England and get back home the same day but he said he drove for three days and was still in Ontario. It's a big country.

Day after day, through wind and rain and sunstroke days they made their way across this great country lugging their duffel bags content with the knowledge that everything they really might need would be in those bags.

They finally stuck their toes in the Pacific and started back to Alberta. They made it. They had seen Canada. It was time to settle in, unpack and embark on their new careers.

If you have bowled ten pin you have hefted a bowling ball. If you have not, try it. Once you have hefted that bowling ball imagine what the weight would feel like if it was one-fifth the size but five times the weight.

That is what our friend found in the bottom of his duffel bag that he had just dragged across Canada. Not a bowling ball but an iron cannonball that his so called friends had dropped into his bag and buried with his socks and underwear.

"I never noticed," said our friend.

A Customs Officer was once purported to have asked a traveler, "Has anyone put anything in your luggage without your knowledge?" Perhaps that wasn't such a dumb question after all. Our friend claims he checks his luggage very carefully. Now.

Meetings

McMaster Hospital in concert with the Juravinski Cancer Centre put a team of Oncologists together to coordinate patient treatment. They are good.

However, for a while, life becomes a series of meetings. Surgery is discussed, carried out, assessed and follow-up meetings are set. Chemotherapy is discussed, assessed, started in some form or another and follow-up meetings are set.

Radiation treatments are discussed, assessed, carried out and follow-up meetings are set.

Every meeting becomes an assessment of weighing benefits against risk.

"What does this do?"

"What happens if we don't do that?"

"How much does that improve the likelihood of knocking this thing back?"

"What are the side effects?"

"How long does it go on?"

"Tell me those percentages again, please?"

"When can we start?"

"How do we monitor the effects?"

The surgeon seems pleased with the report she received. The medical oncologist seems confident that we are on the right track.

The radiation oncologist says to Wanda when she comments that she doesn't need to live until she is 100, "Come back and see me when you're 99." We laugh but we're relieved by his air of confidence.

"Tell me those percentages again, please."

The oncologist tells you that you are more likely to get run down by a car than you will miss out on living a long and happy life because of the treatment they are providing.

It's a relief meeting. There are no happy meetings. You jot down the percentages you were given.

Charlie & Margaret

I knew Charlie Juravinski long before he became Charlie Juravinski. I've never met his wife Margaret but I'm sure she has had her hands full with Charlie over all these many years.

The local newspaper ran an article on Charlie and Margaret pointing out how much they have assisted the development of the cancer treatment facilities on Concession Street, Hamilton Mountain. Charlie and Margaret have donated forty-three million dollars to the facility and continue to support what has become known as one of the best cancer treatment facility in the country.

I first met Charlie when he delivered a section of used pipe to my mother's house for use as a clothes line support. Charlie was a steel salesman, public relations guy and deliveryman. He was, at that time, a short step from the Ukrainian kid who washed vehicles to help him pay his way through school and a long step from the very successful entrepreneur that could support a hospital to the point where it would carry his name.

I watched Charlie build a construction company and then move on from there. I watched him as a curler with the most unorthodox curling style in the history of the game. I watched him run for nomination to political office and lose. After all, who would want a successful business person with a philanthropic streak to hold public office?

I watched him as a tough business person operate Flamborough Downs Racetrack for years and learned of his sale of that endeavor for several million dollars. Then I learned of his donation, apparently very much encouraged by Margaret, to the cancer centre.

Way to go Charlie. Way to go Margaret.

You do a lot of good for a lot of people every day.

I like it when people refer to you as Charlie and Margaret even though you've well earned "Mr. and Mrs. Juravinski".

Decisions

Somewhere along the line, if we live long enough, we get it figured out that life is really just an ongoing selection of choices and that each one of those choices involves making a decision.

We can choose to be obnoxious or not. We can choose to be kind or mean. We can choose to be good or bad. Any one of those choices can be right or wrong. Sometimes both choices can be right and wrong.

One of my good friends once accused me of always choosing to "march towards the sound of gunfire." A nice person who works with me gave me a Christmas gift with her framed comment directed towards me that said "When you go through life starting fires, every now and again you can expect to get burned."

I think that was the same year when I received a card from our office staff that read, "By a vote of five to four the staff wishes you a Merry Christmas."

When I was forced to give up our construction business I was looking to start over at age forty-eight. It was somewhat of a daunting task. As there was very little work available for a forty-eight year old man I accepted a sales role with an insurance company and set out to re-build a way to make a living.

When you're starting out in a new business at that stage of your life and when your friends and former associates learn you are now selling insurance, a lot of phone calls are not returned. Some of your friends become even greater friends. Some disappear.

In order to find new business I used the "Mirror Test" to identify new prospects who might qualify to do business with me. For those of you who have never heard of the "Mirror Test" you hold a mirror up to the mouth of a possible prospective buyer. If the mirror fogs up it indicates they are alive and breathing and are, therefore, a qualified prospect. Deals were hard to find.

Wanda would make contact phone calls for me and set up evening appointments for five nights every week. I would call on the prospects and she would set up another series of appointments. It was hard work, especially when she was also trying to learn the real estate business but it was a decision we needed to make. We were living in a rented house at that time, having had our house foreclosed on us by the bank, so the appointments made the difference between paying the rent and not paying the rent.

Even if it meant that I re-visited the same prospect several times, if it meant a sale the re-visits were made.

I recall one particular situation where there was an obvious family need for what I was proposing. The mother of the family saw the need and was encouraging her husband to make the deal. He would come close to making a decision and then would back off. I would agree to get together again some other time and would re-set an appointment.

After the fourth such meeting where the husband would be almost ready to proceed and backed off again even I, the desperate sales person, had reached the point where I told him that if he ever wanted to proceed he could call me and we would do the deal. Otherwise, I was not interested in coming out to see him again.

His rather disappointed wife walked me to the door and as I was saying my good-byes she said, "Please don't be too disappointed in him. It took him seven years to name the dog."

Some people just find it hard to make decisions.

The Right Thing To Do

Sometimes things just hurt too much to make sense.

Ed was working on the roof of the house that he had literally built with his own hands. He is a landscape architect by trade and a very successful artist well renowned in the Muskoka area. His wife Dawn, a special needs teacher, was working in the kitchen.

A neighbour and very good friend arrived with tears streaming down her face. She told Ed and then Dawn of the murder of their daughter Natalie, a twenty year old student in Toronto. The murder, committed by a person who was under a restraining order, had taken place the night before and through a communications mix-up the police had not informed the family.

The neighbour learned of the killing through a phone call from her daughter who was Natalie's best friend. The killer, after three years of working his way through our legal system, was eventually convicted and sentenced to life imprisonment.

Sometimes things just hurt too much to make sense.

For three years the family grew closer together and also, occasionally, blew further apart. Some things are almost too awful and such things leave people inconsolable. Thus it was for Dawn, Ed, Nick (Natalie's brother) and my sister Alice who was Natalie's grandmother.

It was three years of hearings, investigations, court appearances, counselling and a wild mix of sorrow and anger. Finally, after sitting through absolutely brutal testimony and after listening to the accused explain why he felt he should be allowed to fire his third legal aid lawyer, the trial was over and some form of closure could begin.

The healing process took a huge jump forward when Nick announced that he and Erin were engaged to be married and a wedding date was set in her hometown of Ottawa.

Plans needed to be made and finalized. Distractions from the events of the previous three years were inevitable. Decisions needed to be made. Life was moving on.

Wanda and I were invited to the wedding and I was honoured to be made part of the ceremony. It was a beautiful Ottawa day. Arrangements had been made for a luncheon at an Ottawa restaurant not far from the Church. Wanda and I were assigned seating at the same table as the priest who had performed the ceremony.

I don't know why we drew the table with the priest but I knew my vocabulary, well developed during my years in the construction business, would be reduced by half because of the priestly presence at our table. Wanda reminded me that it should.

During the luncheon chit chat I learned that the priest was a child in Holland during World War II. Anyone who knows even the slightest bit of World War II history knows how difficult it was to survive in Holland. He assured me that they really were reduced to eating tulip bulbs as there was no other food left by the occupying Germans.

I remarked that to this day there seems to be a special place in the hearts of the people of Holland for Canada as the Canadian soldiers were very much in the forefront during the liberation of Holland.

He told me a story.

He and his little brother had been instructed by their parents to immediately run home and tell them if they ever saw any soldiers in uniform anywhere around where they lived. He and his brother were out playing, he was about eight years old at the time, when he saw soldiers coming out of some nearby trees. As instructed, they immediately rushed home and told the parents.

A few minutes later there was a bang bang on the front door and his parents who had been rushing around the house opened the door only to find two Canadian soldiers with big grins on their faces announcing that they were here and Holland was in the liberation stage.

Whoops and cheers and hugs and kisses all around.

Then a family of four appeared from the basement. It seems that mother and father had been hiding a Jewish family in the basement for months and were afraid to even tell their children in case they let something slip. They wanted the warning if there were soldiers in the area as they knew none of them would survive if the family was found.

I asked the priest why his Mom and Dad would have done such a thing with so much being at risk. He thought for a minute and said, "Because it was the right thing to do."

It was a good wedding. Life moves on.

Navy and Notre Dame

Many of our trips were taken in the Fall. As a Canadian one gets the feeling that you need to pay a certain amount of dues and live in a refrigerator for several months each year. This punishment time seems to increase each year as you get older so any thing you can do to extend the nice weather of Autumn or to bring on the good feeling of Spring starts to make more and more sense. A break away in the Fall provides that extension of good weather.

Before my father passed away he passed along a couple of things to me that have been important. I still wear his ring that he earned for something or other many years ago. I still follow his advice that was basically, when you get knocked down the first thing to do is get up and I inherited his respect for Notre Dame University and for their football program.

He told me all about Knute Rockne, the legendary coach. He liked the story about Rockne sneaking into his seven year old son's first communion procession and taking communion as a new convert much to the surprise of his son. I think Dad liked the idea that Notre Dame, a Catholic University, would hire a non-Catholic like Rockne because he was the best football coach they could find. It had nothing to do with religion. I remember lessons like those.

I always followed the team in good years and in bad. A sports does things like that to you. I was a proverbial "die hard" fan of the old Brooklyn Dodgers and have never forgiven them for moving to the west coast. I lived and died with the Boston Red Sox as year after year they managed to snatch defeat from the jaws of victory and please keep this a secret, I still cheer for the Toronto Maple Leafs. I've been pretty good at picking winners in the people area of my life but obviously a slow learner with team sports.

For many years, one of the exceptions to my cheering for losers was the Notre Dame football team. They seem to be less competitive now and I've put that down to the fact that they insist on good academic performance from their players. They wind up playing against a lot of football factories where student football players major in basket weaving 101 rather than keeping high grades in their law and science programs. The military colleges have the same problem.

We attended a fund raising dinner where the organizers offered items for sale at a silent auction. For those who may not know how a silent auction works, the item for sale is put on display and bidders mark their name and the amount of their bid on an attached card. As a bidder you then watch the card and if you are out-bid you can raise your bid amount until the bids are closed. If you have the highest bid on the card you take home your prize and the charity makes some extra money.

My friend came back to our table and announced that he had put my name and a bid on an item offered for sale.

"Shouldn't I have something to say about that?" I asked.

"It was an expensive bid but you'll like it", he said. "Besides, it's for charity."

As I was now a bidder on an expensive item I knew nothing about I thought that I had better check this situation out. I checked out the bid table and found that I had put in a sizeable bid on four football tickets for a game to be played in New Jersey that following Fall between Notre Dame and Navy. I was hooked.

Every fifteen minutes thereafter I got up and checked the bid card to make sure I wasn't being outbid by someone who, in my mind, was not nearly as deserving of those tickets as me. According to the bid card there was another bidder and he outbid me by twenty-five dollars.

I raised that unknown lout by twenty-five dollars. That should settle the issue.

When I next checked the card I found that I was, once again, outbid by twenty-five dollars. My response to that was to raise the bid by fifty dollars in order to put a stop to this nonsense. It was time to relax. Actually, I relaxed for about five minutes then thought that I better check again.

Sure enough, the bid had been raised again by twenty-five dollars.

"If I don't tell Wanda", I thought, "I can raise this another fifty dollars."

That's what I did. I also hung around the bid table until the auction was closed to make sure I could defend my turf and get my tickets. It was some time later when I had the sinking suspicion that the bidder that was driving up my costs was probably my good friend Rick that started the bidding in the first place. That's what friends are for, I guess.

At any rate, I was finally getting the opportunity of seeing a Notre Dame football game even if it was against a team that they had defeated in every game they played against each other for forty-six years.

Although only Wanda and I were going to the game I knew I could sell the two extra tickets outside the stadium with little trouble and I sold them to a ticket scalper just to be rid of the hassle.

The morning of the game we got up early and I told Wanda I had arranged a car and driver to take us into New York City, right across the river, so that we could visit the site of the 911 attack and pay our respects.

It's an awesome and awful sight. The Fire Station that is marked "Station No.1" now also is marked with a plaque that carries the names of all of those very first responders, most of whom were killed that day going up the stairs to try to help someone else.

Fortunately, it seems that there's always someone who will "go up the stairs" no matter the risk.

The football stadium security reflected the change in our lives that came with 911. Bags were opened and inspected. We passed through metal detectors. Security rods that hummed and squeaked were passed over us. Welcome to the new society.

We were in our seats early and I figured out that the persons seated next to me were the ones that bought the tickets from the scalper I had found. Being curious, I asked him how much he had paid for the tickets, after explaining why the question. He told me and I was relieved that no one had made a whole lot of money except the charity that got me in the first place. It turned out the man that bought the tickets was from New York and was here at the game with his nine year old son. It turned out he worked about six blocks from the twin towers and was there the day of attack. He told me he still worked six blocks from ground zero and had never been able to bring himself to even go there and view the site. He'd lost friends.

As the game was starting I heard him ask his son, "Who are you cheering for?"

The son, knowing who was buying the hot dogs and the pennants answered, "I'm not sure. Who are you cheering for?"

"I'm cheering for Notre Dame," he answered. "Your uncle Louie went to Notre Dame so I'm cheering for Notre Dame for his sake."

"Then I'm cheering for Notre Dame too," said the lad. He is obviously ready for politics.

As it was considered to be a Navy home game the halftime show was primarily a Navy show. The full compliment of Navy midshipmen attending the nearby Annapolis Naval Academy, were on display and in formation covering the entire field with their band and precision marching displays. It was spit and polish.

"My Gawd," observed Wanda, "they all look like Richard Gere in that movie An Officer and a Gentleman. This is a good game to come and see."

"Settle down," she was advised.

During World War II the attendance at Universities in the US had fallen off to the point where many of the grand old schools were on the verge of bankruptcy. That appeared to be the situation at Notre Dame.

The US Navy in their search for available training facilities started to use Notre Dame as a major location, working in conjunction with Navy, to complete advanced training. It's believed by many that the assistance from Navy helped save Notre Dame and helped keep it going during a difficult time.

For whatever the reason, Notre Dame which had become a major football power and attraction again after World War II, kept Navy on their football schedule well past the power days and attraction days of Navy football. Notre Dame was often pressured to replace Navy on their schedule as a more renowned opponent might help them in national ratings. Navy stayed on. You don't drop your friends.

It was clear in the first half that Notre Dame had the bigger, better and stronger team. It was clear by late in the second half that the game was well in hand. Late in the game Navy fumbled close to their own goal line and the ball was recovered by Notre Dame.

On the first down Notre Dame ran the ball straight at the best Navy defender. The run was stopped with no gain. On the second down they repeated the play and the results were the same. On the third down Notre Dame ran an end around play that was easily strung out and stopped by Navy. Notre Dame had been stopped and only a field goal ensued.

It was great to watch. Two great institutions tested what they were all about and neither was shown up by the other. You don't forget your friends. There is no need to run up the score. At least that's what I saw.

On the way back to our hotel I asked Wanda what she liked about the game.

"They all looked like Richard Gere," she said.

How Did That Happen

When Wanda was in the real estate business she met some great and wonderful characters. She arrived home from her very first day at the office where she had been assigned the duty phone task. It's a good place for a rookie to start because you get the cold calls from people who may not yet be working with an agent so you get an opportunity to find new clients.

She told me she took a call from someone looking for warehouse storage space. She was pleased that she was able to search the system and find someone who had space immediately available. She called and was put in touch with the owner.

"He was the nicest man", she told me. "He said he would be pleased to meet me anywhere at any time to discuss whatever business I had in mind."

"Who is this guy?" I asked.

She gave me the name of one of the most well known mafia figures in the city.

After the expected, "You're kidding," and my assurances that I was not, she agreed that she should leave that account with a more experienced agent and move on. The very next day she was back with another listing. When I didn't recognize the name we both felt a lot better.

"I listed a house in the west end that the owners had up for private sale. They are building a house in Ancaster and are anxious to sell and move."

As Ancaster is one of the higher end areas of the city and they were moving from a very ordinary neighbourhood, I asked what the owner did that would prompt such an upgrade.

"He's a concrete finisher."

"Wanda, concrete finishers just don't make those kind of moves. There must be something else going on."

"Well, yes. They also just won close to a million dollars in the lottery."

Makes sense to me!

I also got to know them through Wanda and when their old house was sold, Wanda made the sale. They moved into their new fancy place and we were invited for dinner. It was a typical Italian dinner. Their two boys spent the entire evening carrying food from the basement kitchen to us in the dining room. I lost count after the sixth course. The conversation was fun but tinged with a bit of sadness as they explained how they had lost a lot of their friends since the lotto win.

"Everybody we knew wanted money from us", she explained. "Every relative we had wanted money or a loan. If we said no they stopped speaking to us. My husband bought a new car and took it to work. His pals wouldn't talk to him and told him to quit because he was taking somebody else's job. We even went back to Italy for a while but it was worse there."

"Now we stay here and have dinner with new friends."

After dinner we got the house tour led by the husband. When we remarked on the beautiful silver tea set on a sideboard he shrugged, agreed it was nice and moved on.

When we were settled and he had gone for another bottle of his best wine, I think it was the fourth bottle, no it was the fifth, she said, "Let me tell you about the silver tea set."

"I always liked nice things. We were very poor but I saw the tea set on sale. I came home and asked if we could buy it."

"You must be out of your mind", was his answer. "We're hardly able to buy food, and you want to buy a tea set?"

"My birthday is coming," she replied. "Can I just buy the sugar bowl for my birthday?"

He agreed.

Apparently, unbeknownst to her husband she had been squirreling away a little bit of money every week and accumulated a few dollars. She went and bought the complete tea set, put the sugar bowl on the table and hid all the other pieces in their attic.

"Every special time after that, Christmas, Anniversary, Birthday, it didn't matter. I would tell him, don't bother with a present. I will buy another piece of our tea set. I would sneak up into the attic and bring down another piece. Now he gets all puffed up and acts like it's his. I got it done. I got the tea set."

I guess if it's important enough you find a way to get it done.

My friend Ted tells the story of how a plant owned by the company he worked with had received a very important order from the U.S. Air Force. The item was to be built at their Baltimore plant and, to the surprise of almost everyone the contract was completed ahead of schedule and below budget.

The Air Force wanted to recognize the job done by the workforce and, as the Blue Angel precision flying team was scheduled to do a show in the Washington area, the Air Force informed the factory management people that if they were to get their workforce out into the parking lot the following Tuesday at exactly 11:15 in the morning, the Blue Angels would do a low level fly past as a display of thanks.

The word spread like wildfire through the plant and the workers were delighted.

Unfortunately, right at about this point the bean counters otherwise known as the regulators or, by some of us, the empty suits, got into the act.

They announced, probably after returning from a comfortable two martini lunch, that such an incursion by the Blue Angels would be too disruptive to the workday and that everyone would be required to punch out and then punch in again. They also pointed out that the entire plant would need to be shut down for up to half an hour. The fly past was to be cancelled.

Someone, with some authority went to the management people and said, "Leave the fly past the way it's scheduled. Those guys are so precise that if they say they will buzz this plant at 11:15 you can be assured they will buzz this plant at exactly 11:15. Leave the rest to me" he said.

The fly past was left as scheduled. At exactly 11:05 the person who had said, leave it to me", pulled the main fire alarm and the plant workforce emptied into the parking lot. The Blue Angels buzzed the plant. The plant workers waved their thanks. The place went back to work.

Only the empty suits were confused and were left wondering how that happened. Everyone else just gained a lot of additional respect for someone who could think outside the nine dots and who could get it done.

It is kind of interesting to see how you can get it done if you do some thinking. It doesn't matter if you're organizing a tea set or a fly past. There is more than one way to skin the proverbial cat.

Visit With Dad

My father had almost no manual skills and I inherited that from him.

For Christmas I once gave Wanda an electric power drill, at her request, so that she could get some things done around the house. It was of no use to me. For those of you who might think that an electric drill was a strange Christmas gift to your wife I present a real serious Christmas gift mistake.

My brother-in-law Paul asked his wife Laura what she would like for Christmas. Playing the coy and unselfish wife she responded, "Oh nothing". That's what he got her that year.

The following year and for every year thereafter, Laura goes out with credit card in hand and buys whatever she would like to get for Christmas and charges it to Paul. She even has her purchases gift wrapped and placed under the Christmas tree. Paul claims his reaction to her "Oh nothing" answer has cost him thousands of dollars.

That's why when Wanda said she wanted an electric drill that's what I got her. I even paid extra and got her a reversible drill so that she had the top of the line article.

However, getting back to my father's lack of manual skills I watched him, when I was just a wee tad, decide to re-screen our back door. He needed a flat surface to lay the screen door down and to nail the new screen in place. He decided that the kitchen floor was his best bet and proceeded to lay the door down, remove the old torn screen and nail the new screen in place.

His problem was that he used three quarter inch nails and drove them through the half inch wooden door frame, very effectively nailing the screen door to the kitchen floor while my mother watched.

Even at a young age I had survivor instincts that kicked into action. I grabbed the dog and immediately ran to the furthermost point in our back yard and hid as I knew that nothing good was going to happen in the next short while in our house. It was a day of lessons well learned.

My father died of cancer when I was fourteen. He died the day after Remembrance Day and every year since his death I have visited his grave and we have a little mental chat. Being of a Catholic upbringing I've always had this belief, or hope, that one could carry on a mental conversation with someone who has passed on. It doesn't make any sense to hold such a thought but, on the other hand, it's sometimes comforting.

It's not dissimilar to the Catholic sacrament of Confession or Reconciliation as it's now called. The idea of confessing one's identifiable sins to a priest who passes them on to God for forgiveness works for many and provides the penitent with a clean slate. Sometimes you might be better off if you go direct. That's how I wind up chatting with my Dad during my annual graveside visit.

I had told my story about Dad nailing the screen door to the floor in a collection of stories I had written earlier. I had a copy of the book in my car when I made my annual anniversary visit to the gravesite. These visits usually allow me to run a mental report on what has transpired since my last visit and it offers a moment of introspection that I would miss if it didn't take place.

In this particular year the visit took place on a cold, damp and raw November day. The rain was not quite sleet but was getting close. I cut the visit a little short and returned to the car where I sat just thinking about things in general.

I thought of the book in the car and decided I would read Dad one of the stories. I opened the book at random at the story about the nailing of the screen door. I read it aloud to myself and chuckled my way through it. It's a funny memory.

I was no sooner finished the reading when there was a major bolt of lightning and a serious rumble of thunder.

"Come on Dad," I said. "It's only a story. You've got a better sense of humour than that."

Now, I know there is nothing to any of this stuff but I don't read him any more stories during my visits. I haven't run into any electrical storms either during such visits but I still think there's nothing wrong with funny memories. I can only hope that Dad agrees and lays off the lightning bolts.

That made me nervous.

Clubs and Churches

I have never done well in Clubs. I've joined few and lasted for short periods of time when I have been successfully recruited. Before joining any club I believe it's extremely important to know clearly how you can successfully get out of the club.

If there is an over-abundance of pressure brought to bear to get you to join a club it usually follows that it's almost impossible to get out should you choose to do so. The founding members of such clubs have usually made it quite easy for them to oust persons if they become annoyances. Their successors, usually of the same ilk and kind, have seen to it that the removal privilege is also easily available. They have also seen to it that the rules of entry and the rules of expulsion are waived or dramatically eased if the club needs the money that they get from their members.

In other words, most clubs are very often self-serving for those who have elbowed their way to the top. From that point on, the "birds of a feather" syndrome kicks in and even bad or strange behaviour is rewarded by elevation to the inner circle.

Having spoken so churlishly about clubs and their attitudes I know and enjoy some of the comforts that clubs can bring. They can be whatever you wish them to be or they can become whatever you allow them to become. It can support a caste system or it can make a community a better place. It goes way past Rotary or the local Optimists so be careful about joining and make sure you understand why and how you can be thrown out.

By the way, I was a short term member of the local Optimist Club and Wanda was a member of the Optimisses. That meant she was expected to go to the Optimist Hall every Saturday afternoon and serve popcorn to the little darlings that were dropped off at the door by the mothers who wanted to go shop in peace. I just sold peanuts door to door during their bi-annual fund raising drive.

I confess that we are members of a very fine golf club. We enjoy the golf course, the friends we have made, the great dinners we have had with those friends and the association that we have had with them both at and away from the golf course. We stopped attending the annual meetings when it became apparent that we had little, if anything, to say about the running of the golf club. We enjoy the golf course and avoid the puffery.

Attending the annual meeting became more and more difficult for me when Wanda insisted on my agreeing to not refer to some other members as "toffs and swells" and to take the tie she gave me to wear out of my jacket pocket and put it around my neck. It also didn't help my attitude when I concluded that I had not been on the right side of any vote since 1973.

When someone asks why I would join such a club I must admit that I really don't know why but in a perverse way I'm glad I did. When Wanda is brought into the equation, I'm glad that we did. We spend time together and sometimes in life, that gets to be pretty important.

Churches, in their own way, are clubs although the Pope, Mullahs, the Archbishop of Canterbury and perhaps even the Dalai Lama would not admit to the "club" definition being applied to their organizations.

I do know that such places sometimes provide us with an oasis and with an opportunity to look around and perhaps see life through a different prism.

It's delightful to look around and see the new kids and to watch them grow from babies to brides and grooms. It's beautiful to watch the interaction within families and to share their days of congratulations. Sometimes, it gives you the opportunity to help them through difficulties when they might just need to know that they have been noticed. Sometimes it helps to share the hurt, if but just for a moment. Clubs, if taken in the broad sense, can help make that happen.

We've been the recipients of good feelings and you know, it's a good feeling.

We got the telephone calls from the friends we have come to know through those "clubs". The calls came from Florida where, even while they were on a vacation, the thoughts of friends and their encouragement came through. We got the cards. We got the good wishes. We got honest warmth. It came from good caring people that we had met along the way. Sometimes we met them in Clubs or Churches.

I've often cautioned the people I work with to not refer to me as "nice". We kid about it. Then we try to do "nice" things and we watch other people do nice things. It helps you handle it when that wave washes over you and you can't shake off some sadness but then, because good and nice happens to you, you try to pass some of it along to someone else.

I was talking to someone that we knew from Church and thanking her for caring about Wanda. I guess I was just prattling on about how caring about people can form a circle and it helps everyone do better and feel better as they realize they are part of that circle. I told her how many good things had happened to us. I also told her that morning Wanda had gone down to the cancer centre to sit and chat with a friend who was undergoing a lengthy chemo treatment.

She said, "That story gives me goose bumps."

I'm glad.

Clubs and Churches can be okay. All we need to do is let them. It's the people, not the posturing that will always make the difference.

Important Gifts Important Things

We live in a time when all too often our thoughts and sometimes our deeds are driven primarily by what we can buy, have, gain or sometimes steal. We sometimes forget what we know to be really important.

In the world of gifts we sometimes cop out rather than taking the time to come up with that special thing that may remain important forever.

Cash is nice. It's easy and anyone between the age of ten and twenty-five would probably appreciate cash more than just about anything else. One of the great things about cash in that age bracket is that there is no need to feign delight or excitement over the shirt that gramma just sent you for your birthday. Wrong colour, wrong style, wrong designer and probably the wrong size.

A twenty or a fifty dollar bill would have made so much more sense to both gift giver and gift recipient. Maybe next year.

Every year since she came home from the hospital in her mother's arms we gave our granddaughter Kate a music box for Christmas. They started as cartoon characters, moved on through teen romantic characters and on through to young lady depictions that played romantic songs. We stopped the practice when she turned twenty-one because there was no more room on the music box shelves and because life moves on.

Birthdays are a mish-mash of things and of dollars. I can't remember either the gifts or the occasions that prompted the cash or the sweater or the gift certificate nor can the person who received the present. I like to believe, however, that we will all remember the music boxes.

Dan gave me a birthday card that said, "We're Going Fishing". We spent a great afternoon and evening on a river. I can't remember if we caught any fish but I sure remember that afternoon.

Linda had a birthday card framed for me that showed footprints in the sand. The card said, "You're not getting old. You're just going on ahead to check things out for the rest of us."

Tammara, in a difficult year for us, gave me a Snoopy figure doing his Happy Dance. Snoopy has always been one of my heroes. 'Nuff said.

While I was looking for the right play tickets for Wanda or arranging for the outfit she had set aside at her favourite dress shop or buying that electric reversible drill, Wanda found the real important gifts.

The pictures that hung in my parents home re-appeared reframed one Christmas. My father's special watch showed up on a watch stand. This year an antique wall clock that we had bought at an auction on a whim, but was relegated to storage because it never kept proper time, showed up. It still chimes fourteen times several times each day and runs fast or slow whenever it feels like it but it's kind of like me and she knew it. Sometimes it doesn't chime at all but we all know it's there.

I was driving into town the other day and the man on the car radio said' "Think of your greatest dream. Think of the greatest thing that could happen to you."

I immediately thought of how great it would be to stand on an Olympic podium wearing a gold medal while they played the country's National Anthem. The announcer, on the other hand, went on to tell me how much you could win through Saturday's Lotto.

I thought, "Wow I must be really mixed up in my thinking."

But then I thought of another day when I was driving into town and the radio news started to tell the story of that day, September 11, 2001. We all handled it differently.

The one thing that was common that day was that all of the cell phone calls and messages that went out from those buildings to loved ones and family, all talked of love. None talked of gift certificates.

Approximately forty years ago I bought a wrist watch at a good price. Kathy worked for a wholesaler. I wear the watch every day because it tells me the time and, with some assistance, may even tell me the day of the month.

It doesn't tell me the temperature or the altitude or the depth of the pool I'm in at the moment. It just tells me the time but it goes everywhere with me. Because of its age it's getting more difficult to find the proper batteries and to keep it in shape. Perhaps clocks are more like people than we tend to believe.

We found a little jewellery store that had the proper batteries and when the jeweller opened up the watch he declared it was so old and decrepit that it needed a major cleaning and over-haul inside and out. He went on to tell me that he could sell me a brand new watch with even more features for less money than it would cost to over-haul and clean the old watch.

"Will yours come with memories?" I asked.

"We'll get yours cleaned," he smiled.

Smart man.

Time is so important and is probably our most important gift. Hopefully though, we'll also always remember the music boxes and enjoy both.

Mealtime

Wanda has always been the major domo and chef when it comes to our mealtime. From time to time I will be thoughtless enough to comment on the ever increasing number of times we eat out. She reminds me that if I multiplied the number of meals per day times the number of days in the years we've been married the answer would blow up an Apple Computer.

I know if I ask the question, "What did you make for dinner?" the answer is more and more likely to be, "Reservations".

In the summertime I can sometimes lobby successfully for a barbeque dinner provided it's limited to a beer can chicken and a salad for which she has already made the dressing. I am basically relegated to watching and yelling warnings when the smoke gets too thick.

She's really a good cook so I say the long apprenticeship she has served has worked well for me and I have learned to do better with set-up and clean-up.

In the very early days of our marriage we spent time with three other couples and took turns eating at each other's homes. This made sense because none of us had enough money to eat out at restaurants so it became a bit of a cook-off with our friends. Wanda was not all that confident about her cooking skills at that point and was successfully avoiding or delaying our turn to host. That can only go on for so long.

Eventually she was convinced that she had to deal with it being our turn and the friends were invited over for that Saturday night. I had done some pre-positioning with them and had warned them that Wanda was totally inept in the kitchen and that if they were wise they should have a sandwich before they came to our place.

Although I have told Wanda a million times that I don't exaggerate, I may have over-embellished the lack of cooking skills problem, especially as I knew they would be in for a great meal. Wanda, as always had it just right.

The Chateaubriand was perfect. The vegetables were crisp but not over-done. The soup was hot with just a touch of lemon. The home-made pies, there was a choice of two, were great. The Hawaiian coffee was a treat.

The only cheating that took place was done by me. I had worked at the Royal Connaught Hotel at one point and knew the chef. He accommodated my request for a bottle of his famous Sauce Bernaisse that we used to touch up the Chateaubriand.

They all knew they had been set up. Russ was particularly annoyed because he had fallen so far for my story that he admitted to having had a baloney sandwich before he came to our place and that held him to only two helpings of Chateaubriand and only one piece of pie.

Russ was a duck hunter and skeet shooter. I had no idea what skeet shooting was all about. He explained it was target shooting and that skeet was not another species of duck such as Teal. He went on to tell us that Teal was a tough little bird and that only a few people in the world knew how to cook it. He claimed he happened to be one of those people.

He had to tell us how it was done and according to Russ this is how you cook Teal:

Take the eviscerated Teal and nail it to a cedar plank.

Set the plank out in the sun for two to three hours.

Take the planked Teal and throw it into boiling water along with plenty of salt and keep it on high boil for five hours.

After five hours remove the planked Teal from the boiling water, throw away the Teal and eat the plank.

We had strange friends. We agree though, that there aren't too many things that are more fun than sitting around a dining table and telling lies with friends.

Yes, I do help out with the clean-up and yes, I do know where the dishwasher is located. I just don't know how to turn the darn thing on.

Movie Time

We have friends who make a point of seeing almost every new movie of any renown. Don't call them on "Oscar Night" as they will be glued to the presentation of awards and arguing over the choices of the voters and making a case for their own choices as well.

We have not been movie people but we can see the emotions that movies bring to the surface with many people. When the emotions break through there is no stopping them. There is no real holding them back.

It started with Bambi. Who wasn't moved when Bambi's mother was killed by the bad hunters? Of course children were traumatised. Of course many of us grew up hating hunters and hunting. They killed Bambi's mother and you don't get over that very easily.

My friend Gord still mists over when you remind him that "Old Yellar" had to be put down after he contracted rabies while saving the little children. Gord retired some years ago at age fifty but you don't leave things like that behind.

Tammara came home from a date when she was eighteen and found me watching an old movie on television.

"Come in and watch this with me," I suggested. She did. The movie was "The Pride of the Yankees" and it was about Lou Gehrig.

"It's a baseball movie," she protested when she saw what I was watching.

"Not really," I argued. "It's a life story. It's not just about baseball and baseball players."

"It's in black and white," she exclaimed.

"That's okay. Just stay with it," I told her.

When Gehrig, having been stricken with ALS, made his speech in Yankee stadium at his retirement day and told his fans, "Some people say I got a bad break but today, I think I'm the luckiest man on the face of the earth," it was no longer a baseball movie shot in black and white. It was an emotional blow out. Tammara cried that night and has cried every other of the twenty-three times she watched the movie.

Her record of twenty-three viewings of a movie has been topped only by Vickie's thirty-four viewings of the movie Rudy which is about a kid wanting to play football for Notre Dame. When I called their house the other day I asked Dan what Vickie was doing.

"She's watching Rudy for the thirty-fourth time," he answered. "And she's crying for the thirty-fourth time."

"Ghost" - Patrick Swazie.

"We'll always have Paris"- Bogart.

"Where do we get such men?"- Frederick March, the Admiral in Bridges of Toko Ri.

Linda and I went to see "Field of Dreams" For those of you who don't know the movie, it's about a father returning to a mystical baseball field. The closing scene depicts the ghost of his father, who had died many years before, and his once estranged son quietly playing catch. When the lights came up Linda pointed out that the older gentleman sitting in front of us was still just sitting there, sobbing. Something had touched a chord.

It happens.

Sometimes emotions just roll over you and when that wave hits you can't really do much about it and that's okay.

Friends of ours described an acquaintance who absolutely loved movies. He would load himself up with the largest bucket of popcorn that he could buy. He would also buy the largest sized pop that was sold and sit contentedly with both and enjoy a full afternoon or evening at the movies.

There was a particularly emotional movie doing the rounds and this person, fearing that he would have problems containing his emotions, delayed and delayed going to see the film.

Finally, after the movie had been around for a while he felt that he could brave the film and off he went. As was his practice, he loaded up with his popcorn and his soda pop and settled in the third row of an almost empty theatre.

The film moved along and reached a particularly emotional point. Our movie watcher, having consumed most of a large soda pop had also just reached a particularly critical point. He had to go to the washroom but he couldn't bring himself to leave the movie at such a climactic place.

What do you do?

He looked around and spotted the recently emptied popcorn container. You know the rest.

Relieved in more than one sense of the word he settled back into the movie. Unfortunately for him the movie became even more emotional and, coincidentally, the affect of the large soda pop had not finished with him.

Again he could not leave the film. Again he looked around. Again he spotted the popcorn container. Unfortunately for him the designers of the popcorn container had used a very ordinary quality cardboard because, as far as they knew, the container was being designed to hold only popcorn. Again, you know the rest.

The ensuing mess, including a badly stained trouser pant leg, caused our friend's friend to back his way out of a side door once the house-lights in the theatre were turned up. Hopefully it also taught him that if you are attending a movie that you just can't leave, you better only order a small soda pop or stay away from emotional movies.

Raggedy Ann

Anyone who has ever attended a costume party remembers it. Most times the memories that come with it are pleasant and stories are told with a laugh. It seems that putting on a costume usually brings out a lighter side and causes a lot of inhibitions to disappear, if only for a little while.

Putting on that costume also allows us to be someone we are not. In some situations, putting on a costume allows us to truly be who we are or who we might like to be.

We had a costume party at our home one time. We had a Bishop, three Draculas, the Wicked Witch from the North, a Hockey Player and a well known football player who arrived wearing a pink tutu and smoking a cigar. At six foot three, he made an impression.

Hospitals are not much fun. Unless you are a medical professional or staffer you just don't want to go there. Stay away if you can. The Juravinski Cancer Centre is located on a narrow but busy street on Hamilton Mountain. It's a very busy street.

In fact, when discussing Wanda's prognosis, one of the oncologists commented that she should respond to treatment and she is just as likely to be run over trying to cross the street in front of the centre as she is likely to not respond to treatment.

One of the things we have noticed in crossing that street is the courtesy of the drivers in that area. In a world of meanness on the roads, stoplight runners and tailgaters, it seems that drivers know that persons crossing that street to go in or out of the cancer centre are not having a really good day. The courtesy level goes up. Cars stop and drivers wave you across.

Thanks.

I have always found people watching to be a great recreational sport. Sometimes the spectators are much more interesting than the game. The passengers are more interesting than the trains and airplanes and the audience more interesting than the stage players. It's a great way to spend time and it can usually be done at no cost.

When you are dealing with cancer treatment you do a lot of waiting. The waiting is usually caused because the doctors, nurses and technologists are too busy with too many people. They are really part of the real warrior team. They lose too often through no fault of their own but they win a little more and a little more often every day. It's a sad joke when you hear the television announcer describe a golfer's shot over a pond as "a brave shot". If you really want to see brave, go to a hospital and watch the professionals and their patients. That's where you'll see "brave", not on a golf course.

As a people watcher I have learned over the years that one should watch everyone else in the room if a good looking or handsome person walks in. That's fun.

We were placed in a rather full waiting room while Wanda waited her turn to be called for tests. Every chair was filled and every person in that room was worried. You could read every face and none told good stories.

The waiting room was located adjacent to a main corridor and was separated from the corridor by a solid glass partition. My back was to that partition.

I heard someone knocking on the glass behind me. When I looked I saw two young ladies dressed in what I saw as Raggedy Ann costumes. They had wild fright wigs on and wore red clown noses. Their cheeks were over painted with wild red rouge.

They were smiling and waving. Every person in our waiting room saw them. Every person in our waiting room, for just that moment, smiled. What a gift. Two strangers.

I have no idea who those persons are and I have no idea whether they are staff or volunteers. I do know that every person in that room was lifted, if only for a moment, by two people in costumes who were really showing their true selves. Please keep it up.

I hope someone is telling them how great they are, especially on those afternoons while you wait for test results.

Think Good Thoughts

At one time or another we have all laughed at what might be referred to as "gallows humour". We say things like, "no one ever gets out of life alive" or " where there's a Will there's relations".

It's true. Both of those comments and all those like them are true. It's only when we get slapped with an absolute that clearly shows that life is finite that we feel the enormity of the information.

It's only then that we may start to make "thought" decisions.

We have had the great fun of doing things with people we felt were good people and liked the idea that they too put us in that category in their worlds. As far as we're concerned it's a great compliment to whatever we've been or are likely to be.

We tell stories on ourselves, on our friends and to our friends. I suppose that's why we are still friends. We have wonderful memories and have every intention to make more.

When people ask me about Wanda I tell them, "She's okay. She's a tough lady. We'll be okay".

I hope these stories have been fun. Some have been shadowed by events but the memories and thoughts associated with the tales, for the most part, have been fun and have been good thoughts.

I'm so glad that so many people have taken the time to speak with Wanda and to encourage her on her journey. Their mere presence marks them as winners. I'm grateful that the medical warriors are "out there" and are trying every day.

I'm grateful to my friends and family that have cut me some slack at the right times and that have let me yip and yap on at other times.

I'm grateful to the Raggedy Anns who I have never met.

I'm grateful to Charlie and Marg who have worked so hard to help provide the facilities that help so many people.

You wake up and the thought of what you are dealing with is the first thing that pops into your head. Someone once told me the story of a person who decided to quit smoking. He had been off the weed for six years. He was asked if he still ever thinks about smoking and he, in turn, told this story.

"I've been off smoking for six years. Two weeks ago I was out fishing by myself and I needed to go to the bathroom. I put the fishing pole down, unzipped my fly and was relieving myself over the side of the boat. At that exact moment a fish hit my line. I made a leap for the fishing pole and caught my most intimate parts in the oar-lock. At that point, for about thirty seconds, I didn't think about smoking."

I don't know whether or not that story is true but it does make a point.

When Wanda was taking radiation treatments we would go to the Juravinski Centre together and I would wait. I struck up a conversation with a lady who had her eighty year plus husband taking his radiation hits. As these treatments run for several consecutive days you get to see the same people and you know you are a member of a club that no one wants to join.

We had watched a little eight or nine year old girl finish her treatments and joined with the delight shown by the technologists towards her when she thanked them for doing what they did. The techs applauded her and exchanged high fives with her. They gave her the mask that she needed to wear during her treatments. She was taking it to her school for "show and tell".

My eighty year old lady friend and her husband finished their treatments a day before we finished ours. I wished them luck.

As they walked away I suggested, "Think good thoughts".

They agreed.

Think good thoughts.